CRITICISM

by the same author

MUSIC SURVEY: NEW SERIES 1949–1952
(Edited by Donald Mitchell and Hans Keller)

1975 (1984 MINUS 9)
(reissued as MUSIC, CLOSED SOCIETIES AND FOOTBALL)

STRAVINSKY SEEN AND HEARD

THE GREAT HAYDN QUARTETS

CRITICISM

by
Hans Keller

Edited and with
an Introduction by
JULIAN HOGG

faber and faber
LONDON · BOSTON

First published in 1987
by Faber and Faber Limited
3 Queen Square London WC1N 3AU

Photoset by Parker Typesetting Service Leicester
Printed in Great Britain by
Mackays of Chatham Ltd Kent
All rights reserved

© Mrs Milein Keller, 1987
Introduction and additional material © Julian Hogg, 1987

*This book is sold subject to the condition that it shall not, by way of trade
or otherwise, be lent, resold, hired out or otherwise circulated without the
publisher's prior consent in any form of binding or cover other than that
in which it is published and without a similar condition including
this condition being imposed on the subsequent purchaser.*

British Library Cataloguing in Publication Data

Keller, Hans
Criticism.
1. Musical criticism
I. Title
780'.1'5   ML3880
ISBN 0–571–14802–6
ISBN 0–571–14803–4 Pbk

Contents

Acknowledgements

I should first of all like to express my thanks to the author's widow, Milein Cosman, not only for having entrusted me with the task of preparing the manuscript for publication, but also for her constant help and encouragement; she has generously given much of her time both in searching for material and in making suggestions on reading the typescript. I am also enormously grateful to both Leo Black and Misha Donat for the advice they gave on the many questions I asked them; one crucial instance of Leo Black's help is further acknowledged in the Appendix. My thanks are also due to Dr Anthony Storr, Dr John Dingley, and Paul Hamburger for their help on specific points raised with each of them; to Patrick Carnegy of Faber and Faber for his encouragement and advice; to John Ferguson, Michael Parker, and Philip Tagney for their constructive comments on reading the typescript; to Anne Rice for help at the proof-reading stage; and to my wife, Ann, for her invaluable assistance throughout.

I should also like to acknowledge the *Guardian*, for giving their permission to reproduce the review on p.56 and the *Frankfurter Allgemeine Zeitung*, the original publishers of the author's Cosima Wagner's *Diaries* review, his translation of which appears on p.97. The letter from Benjamin Britten on p.27 is © 1987 The Britten–Pears Foundation and reproduced by permission of the Trustees. It is not to be further reproduced without written permission.

Introduction

Hans Keller died in November 1985, almost nine years after completing this book. It remained unread for that length of time simply because of the author's own reluctance to devote further time preparing it for publication; he began an article on criticism which appeared in *Music and Musicians* just a year before his death with the following paragraph:

> Upstairs in my study lies a finished book under the above title; its prospective publisher keeps imploring me to have it typed – for which purpose, however, I'd have to read close on 100,000 words in order to correct some of them, and the trouble with me is that I'm always passionately interested in my future tasks, never in what I have completed.

In fact, the author 'corrected' very little in my experience, which, as a friend and colleague, spanned the last twenty years of his life; he possessed such remarkable clarity of thought that however extended and complex, his sentences would emanate so fluently as to render any drafting or substantial revision quite unnecessary. This facility was equally apparent whether he was writing or speaking, and his unmistakable voice is clearly audible throughout the book, most of which he wrote while on a three-week holiday. It was beautifully handwritten in large loose-leaf pads, on the covers of which he noted, incidentally, and perhaps not surprisingly to those who knew of his many and varied interests, the results of three Spanish football matches (plus goal-scorers) he'd seen on his hotel television!

Editing has been kept to an absolute minimum and, apart from the typing, the work needed to prepare these pages for publication has involved checking the author's footnotes, researching those which he had indicated but hadn't completed, and adding a few of my own – of an updating nature; making several minor corrections to the text, usually where an obvious 'slip of the pen' had occurred; and (in spite of the author's edicts contained within on the subject of editing!) three or four instances where I have, tremblingly, rewritten a short passage in an attempt at clarification. In addition, there were three occasions where material the author had intended to use was unfortunately unavailable: the solutions to these problems are given in a brief appendix, so as not to litter the pages with overlong, explanatory footnotes.

The first half of the book draws almost entirely on the author's vast, personal experience in relevant fields of activity; a glance at the contents page shows the diverse occupations which he groups together under the provocative heading 'Phoney Professions', and into most of which he had himself plunged 'wholemindedly', as he might have put it. He was a man of awe-inspiring intellectual energy and courage, and constitutionally incapable of, to use another of his favourite inelegant words, 'loafing'. One of his aphorisms makes this point in typically humorous and challenging fashion: 'People spend most of their time and psychological energy on not doing something; the really busy ones are capable of not doing two or three things at the same time. If they only knew that if they reversed that policy, they could live two or three lives instead of none.'

Hans Keller's profound knowledge of the disciplines of music, philosophy, logic, and psychology was, in sum, perhaps unrivalled, and is much in evidence in the argument developed throughout the second half of the book. It is a matter of immense personal sadness for me that he is no longer around, not only because I have been unable to consult him regarding my work on this book, but more importantly, because he is unable to participate in the 'lively' discussions which will undoubtedly ensue and which he would have so hugely enjoyed.

JULIAN HOGG

Hans Keller: A biographical note
by Julian Hogg

As musician and writer, Hans Keller had established himself as a prominent figure in British musical life within ten years of his escape in 1938 from Nazi-ridden Vienna at the age of nineteen. A highly gifted string player, he had worked as a freelance musician in various orchestras, and played the violin and viola with the Adler and Hültenbach Quartets; he had been music adviser to the British Film Institute, and his numerous writings had been published in every type of journal at home and abroad – articles which covered not only a vast range of musical subjects, but psychology as well.

By the time he became Joint Editor with Donald Mitchell of the influential *Music Survey* in 1949, he had already earned himself the reputation among some fellow critics as the bad boy of the profession, thanks to his fearless defence of great music or performance which occasionally necessitated what were seen as attacks on his colleagues.

During the fifties and sixties, he developed his wordless method of music analysis, 'Functional Analysis', in which he composed solely musical demonstrations to illuminate the unity behind contrasting ideas within and between the movements of a composition. Some of these were commissioned and broadcast by the BBC and North German Radio.

In 1959 he joined the BBC's Music Division, and for twenty years was successively in charge of Music Talks, Chamber Music and Recitals, Orchestral and Choral Music, and New Music; his efforts in this last field being officially acknowledged by way of a presentation from the Composers' Guild of Great Britain. For over ten years he was chairman of the working party of European Radio Heads of Music which planned the EBU's International Concert Seasons.

His reputation as musician, writer, lecturer, broadcaster, and

teacher became worldwide – over a dozen compositions are dedi-
cated to him, including Benjamin Britten's Third String Quartet –
and, after his retirement from the BBC, he was Visiting Professor
of Music at McMaster University in Canada, where he also undertook a lecture tour, and teacher of chamber music at both the
Yehudi Menuhin School and the Guildhall School of Music and
Drama; he gave occasional lectures at foreign and British festivals,
as well as at Cambridge and other British Universities and Col-
leges. Until 1985, he was invited annually to the internationally
renowned Summer School of Music at Dartington where, for over
twenty years, he had conducted master classes, analysis classes, and
lectured.

He married the artist Milein Cosman, with whom he col-
laborated on several publications, including *Musical Sketchbook*, and
two volumes on Stravinsky; the only full-length book to appear in
his lifetime, *1975*, included her 'Prague Sketchbook'. Since his
death in November 1985, *The Great Haydn Quartets* has been published, and in a year or two, his book on the Mendelssohn Violin
Concerto will also be published. Shortly before Hans Keller's
death, the President of Austria awarded him the 'Ehrenkreuz für
Wissenschaft und Kunst, 1 Klasse', a cross of honour for his ser-
vices to art.

Preface

It is 25 November 1976, 5.45 a.m. In an hour's time, I shall be flying on a three weeks' holiday with my wife – to a small Canary Island where we work and swim; I know by now that in such surroundings, with no interruptions and the sun to stimulate, I write 3,000 words a day, which means that this book will be finished when we come back on 16 December – all the more reliably so since I am cheating twice over: for one thing, I have now started this Preface well before time, and for another, more important thing, Part III, Section 2 (pp. 134ff.) is actually finished. I wrote it in the past few days because the Editor of *Soundings* wanted an essay by the end of November and I thought I might kill one bird with two stones. But, for the duration of the present book, this will have proved the last act of journalism in which I shall have indulged.

Now, the only other person I know of who liked most of all writing in the sun, and near water, was Bedřich Smetana, who habitually went down to the Vltava to compose. You can hear the sun in his music, rather exceptionally so: music is not a sunny art, and Schubert is said to have remarked that all music was sad when, at a party, a girl asked him to play something jolly. The reader may be relieved to learn that my implication is not that I'm as good as Smetana, but rather that our sun worship may point to temperamental affinities; in fact, whether it points to them or not, they are there. For just as Smetana's musical sadness is, paradoxically, sunny, so, I humbly submit, is my notorious aggression. In a book on criticism, i.e. on one of the most respected sublimations of Freud's *Thanatos*, his death instinct, this observation carries more than mere autobiographical significance. Nor do I pose as a sunny critic. On the contrary, I am aggressively, yet sunnily critical of the respectability of music criticism: anybody who considers reading the present book had better know this at the outset, had better receive a clear statement of bias at the earliest possible moment. It is my long-standing view* that any investigation that aspires to being objective must be based on a clear definition of the author's prejudices – though there may, in fact, be nothing wrong with them. But even in that case, the wrong-headed reader must be given a chance to find something wrong with them, and in the case of a prejudice, however well founded, against a respected cultural activity there will, of necessity, be plenty of wrong-headed people who will find something wrong with it – otherwise the activity would not have survived into a senile old age: music criticism is the grand old manliness of the musical world and, one or two recent honourable exceptions apart, music critics but rarely retire. On the contrary, once they are aged – like Ernest Newman was, an impressive mind that was not terribly musical, or like the slightly more youthful Richard Capell – they are unassailable.

Why, at the same time, I am allowing myself to call my critical attitude towards music criticism sunny is not merely that some of my best friends have been music critics, but that I have come to understand that the need to criticize, and/or to have and see things criticized, is so elemental, so inescapable psychologically, that the musician has to forgive the critic the way religious people forgive original sin. In short, we can't all be critics of critics – although frankly, a few more of us could be, which, as will presently be concretely seen, is one of the reasons, and by no means the least fruitful, why this book is being written.

Once, then, one has realized that there are people, a lot of people, who would rather go hungry than not criticize, it is no longer possible, scientifically or ethically, to consider the problem of music criticism in isolation, without reference to the problem of criticism as such. Nor indeed is it possible to examine any problem without acknowledging one's own part in it, and once one has seen that one spends almost as much time on fruitless criticism, silent or explicit, as do those whose sterile conversations one abhors, one turns all sunny, especially when one actually sits in the sun and the sterilely critical conversations are at a safe, if audible distance.

It is only then that one fully experiences the problem of criticism

---

*See my *1975 (1984 minus 9)*, London, 1977, pp. 84ff. and pp. 141ff. (Reissued under the title *Music, Closed Societies and Football*, London, Toccata Press, 1986. Ed.)

and becomes alive to the fact that in the long history of human thought, the constant compulsion to criticize has never yet been fully appreciated – never yet been as much as named and described. The fact hits one like a revelation, albeit an unpleasant one, and if, at the same time, one has acquired some subtle skills of uncriticism, of being able to do without criticism – and, subsequently, without the withdrawal symptoms of an all-forgiver – one is, I think, in a position to try and tackle the problem and see what happens.

In one respect, at least, I am in a unique position, uniquely qualified for the task before me. Throughout my writing and speaking life, I have been reproached with my aggressively critical behaviour, but not once has anybody noticed, at least in public, that the only thing I have been aggressively critical of has been criticism – manifestly or latently aggressive, as the case may be. Time and again, what I had intended as a defence – of those criticized – was taken as an attack on the critics. The one doesn't exclude the other, of course; in fact, while there is plenty of attack which does not involve simultaneous defence, there is no defence without attack. Now, when I have been attacked because of my attacks, the real or intended victim of any attack on me has always been somebody or something I had defended, yet these attacking acts of aggression, as opposed to my defensive ones, have remained unnoticed. It is thus that I have learnt that whether somebody is regarded as aggressive or peaceable, 'critical' or 'understanding' does not altogether depend on whether he is aggressive or peaceable, critical or understanding. Far be it from me to deny my aggression, but those whom I have attacked in defence of something or somebody have almost invariably been more aggressive than I, more 'critical' than I. However, their object of aggression and of criticism was traditionally legitimate, i.e. art, and mine was illegitimate, i.e. criticism. It followed, you understand, that they were peaceable and reasonable, whereas I was aggressive and, outside my undoubted musical competence, a shade irrational, adolescent, showy, and the rest. I was thus offered unique, first-hand insight, not just into what social and professional conventions can do to human character but, more important, what they can do to human assessment of human character. My appetite for assessment had thus been spoilt for a long time, perhaps for ever – and what remains of a critic without the passion to assess?

'Dog does not eat dog' I was publicly warned, early on, by the then anonymous Music Critic of *The Times* who has now secured himself a dark niche in the dusky history of music criticism, and who was a fool. I hadn't, alas, eaten him; I had merely demonstrated his incompetence and the way it harmed our art. That was the man who propounded that Schoenberg was not a composer at all, even though he had to be acknowledged as a seminal influence. Our Music Critic's negative discovery was greeted with applause on the one hand and minority silence on the other; only I decided upon a defensive counter-attack – and was, thenceforth, not a proper member of the profession.

Another critic, almost equally elevated, drew attention to a different side of my unprofessional behaviour – my close professional relations with certain leading artists, such as Benjamin Britten and indeed Schoenberg (whom, in fact, I never met, though everybody came to assume that I knew him intimately). I was reminded that I had personal relations – all professional relations that are disliked are considered personal – with the wrong kind, the wrong category of people. With most critics, on the other hand, I was hardly on speaking terms – or rather, they weren't with me, for I have never felt any personal hostility towards people the validity of whose work I am unable to acknowledge. Anyhow, this distinguished music critic pronounced with ethical revulsion that I was in close personal touch with artists about whose work I wrote: how could I hope to arrive at an objective assessment of their art? It was at this stage that the unshakeable dream-world which a profession – especially an intrinsically aggressive profession – tends to create for itself struck me so violently that, for ever after, I was to become suspicious of all ethical realities which any group accepted without internal friction. For in the same week in which my supremely ethical senior colleague had publicly reprimanded me, he published an effusively favourable review of a lousy book by a fellow critic, a close friend of his: dog does not eat dog, especially when dog knows dog jolly well and, in any case, doesn't want to be eaten himself on any future occasion.

For a long time in my twenties and early thirties, I was determined to write a book on music criticism – on what music criticism was, what it should be instead, how it could serve rather than inhibit the art of music. I was in dead earnest, or thought I was. The book had been publicly announced; a leading publisher had paid me a handsome advance on royalties. I collected an enormous amount of material, consisting of sundry palpable anti-models, but although I have always been a very quick writer and know of no other working inhibition in my life, I never wrote a single line of that book, and eventually returned the money to the publisher. The facts were, simply, that although I knew very well what music criticism was, I did not know what it should be; and although I was happy about my own criticisms when they contributed insight, I was unhappy about them when I could not see the concrete purpose of unfavourable remarks, general or specific, critical of works or of performances: whom did one serve, and how? The artist would be depressed by public exposure, and as for educating the public, that could only happen realistically, specifically, if listeners could hear that which one had criticized after they had read one's review instead of before – or, better, after as well as before. With a few exceptions, this consideration reduced fruitful but unfavourable reviewing to opera, the gramophone record, and film music.

For a time, I took these limitations very seriously – though it must be said that I merely *concentrated* on the repeated and repeatable rather than *confining* myself to it so far as negative criticism was concerned: too often – or perhaps just often enough – sheer musical interest, even where it was purely negative, gained the upper hand over musico-sociological considerations. Besides, I never was an opera fan – about twenty-five musically supreme masterpieces in this curious medium apart – and though I went to the trouble, very early on, of writing a pamphlet on *The Need for Competent Film Music Criticism* for the British Film Institute,* film music could never become more than an artistic side-line for me. As for the gramophone record, I have always hated it as an anti-musical invention, with its deadening influence on both performance (mistakes must be corrected by retakes) and listening (the uniqueness of performance is abolished).

For the rest, I had always gravitated towards analysis rather than criticism anyway, and once I had started to teach, composition as well as string-quartet playing, I came to grasp the violent difference, in the effect on the artist, between a critical remark made to him in private and a critical remark made in public about him – even though the essence of the remark, and the artist too, might be the same in either situation. And so I eventually decided to retire

*London, 1947.

from criticism as we know it, and though I continued to be known as a critic or, still worse, a musicologist, my passport rightly says that I am a musician and a writer. Well, now, if I could not solve the problem of criticism for myself, what right had I to solve it for others? Would I not turn into the type of teacher, of which we shall hear more later on,* I loathed most – the man whose material for solving his own difficulties were other people?

The sun, never quite hidden behind the clouds (many of them, admittedly, threatening), now began to break through after all. While my respect for the work of most critics did not increase, my appreciation of their difficulties did, most of them inherent in the critical situation, and in both its sociological and its psychological aspects.

I did not repress my problems; I carefully and findably filed them, and down the years, more and more were added to the files. Critics of sovereign competence – say, masterly composers them-selves – made fools of themselves as easily as did those who were musically ill-equipped; they tried to make fools of their peers, too, verbally obstructing the very art to whose development they had devoted their lives. Indeed, composers identified with pitiable critics just because these nitwits happened to hate the same people or works as they did; if, on the other hand, the selfsame critics happened to *love* the same works, the composers soon found them out – found little, or many wrong things, behind the critics' love, and didn't identify with them: common hate is easy, but common love isn't. Common hate is usually based on joint incomprehen-sion, whereas common love, just as usually, is comprehension joined to incomprehension: the only thing that is far easier than to love for the wrong reasons is to hate for the wrong reasons; in fact, it is doubtful that if not so many wrong reasons were available, much hatred would remain. Or, to put it less fancifully, more soberly from the psychological point of view, there is no limit to the possible rationalizations and, worse, moralizations of hatred; more of this when the time comes.†

Meanwhile, let me gradually work down to the end of my Preface by stressing that the more I came to turn my back on criticism, the more I turned my front on it as it were, attempting to

---

*See pp. 72ff.
†See Part II, pp. 89ff.

face the psychological and sociological problems that surrounded criticism like concentric circles, as well as the central, insoluble problem of criticism itself. Or was it only because I was a musician that I regarded the problem of music criticism, or of art criticism generally, as central? Was it this problem that was itself one of the concentric circles, and not an inner circle either, and did the centre of it all lie elsewhere – a centre equally unsolvable, if not indeed intractable on a purely intellectual level?

And so I went round and round, year in, year out – but not, I hope, in circles. Rather, I devised a new type of merry-go-round for myself – a merry-go-up which, I fondly thought, ascended in a spiral, until I reached, not perhaps a solution, but at least clear insight, the clearer for the problems now being sunlit, up there over the clouds.

I don't, in fact, think that it is difficult to discover when you have reached that minimum of insight which entitles you to bother other people with it, be it in a pub, a lecture, or a book: I do not, in ethical principle, make any difference, for either you take the responsibility for communicating what you, at least, have firmly come to regard as the truth, or you don't – and if the psychological circumstances happen to obtain, you can, in fact, have a far more decisive influence on two or three people in a pub than on two or three hundred in a lecture hall, or on fifty or a hundred thousand in a radio studio, or on two or three millions in a television studio that aims at the messiest mass consumption. The people who chide me for not showing sufficient respect for the mass media seem to forget that what they, by implication, call the masses, and what I call a great number of different people, listen to me far more attentively, and in far greater numbers, than they listen to them as individual 'communicators', if they listen to them at all. The reason is not that I am that much more marvellous than they are (though, in all conscience, that shouldn't be difficult to achieve), but that throughout my life, I have regarded the (self-invented) Eleventh Commandment as, intellectually, the most important of the lot: Thou shalt know when to shut up, and once you do know, people will listen when you don't shut up, for they will sense your initial respect for them, will sense that you refuse to bother them before you have reached what, for you at least, is minimal insight.

And it isn't all that difficult to know when you have reached that point, in that nothing is easier than to compare an allegedly insightful mental state with a mental state of proven insight – say, into twice two making four, or (to approach the present complications of this book a little more closely) into twice seventy-nine minus one and a half amounting to one hundred and fifty-six and a half: you don't need any books, notes, drafts and sketches in order to arrive at the latter conclusion, for the simple reason that you have got the means towards gaining and communicating this piece of insight well inside you; and if you make a mistake, it will be incidental, not essential, and proportionately reparable once it is pointed out to you.

There may be one or the other reader who has heard me speak in public. He will have noticed that I despise *all* types of 'aids'. Scripts I never used: you either write or you talk, and each mode of communication has its own functional character. Any kind of 'lecture notes', likewise, I dispensed with many years ago – nor indeed have I been using scores for the past decade or so: the more specific a lecture about music, the more important it is to have not only what one has to say completely inside one, but, of course, also the music about which one says it. Otherwise, one simply cannot be sure that one's insights have reached minimal intensity and minimal clarity.

Of course, it being well inside you does not prove you right, but it not being well inside you easily proves you wrong or, at the very least, not as clear as you could be – as you are in the case of twice seventy-nine minus one and a half. And whenever you communicate without being as clear as you could be, and especially if you purport to communicate truth or right, it's not merely an imposition – it's a crime, minor or major according to the circumstances of your communication and its substance; but in any case, it's worse than stealing a loaf of bread, because the harm you do, or the good you omit to do, may well have more than a temporary effect.

So there we are. I have not come to the Canaries with a trunk full of books or scores, or with a folder full of notes. The only note I have is the sentence I wrote down when I had lunch with my publisher* and asked him whether he would publish this book if I wrote it and he said yes. It is the opening sentence of Part II; I then thought it would open the book. Otherwise, I have come with my thoughts on the problems of criticism which, I trust, have reached

---

*(Not the present publisher. Ed.)

the minimum of insight necessary for disclosure. Above all, they have reached the stage that succeeds the one where you save the world – the stage where truth-finding is more important than world-saving, and where problems are not denied, or ignored, or neglected just because one can't offer any solution, or because one realizes, in fact, that there is no solution. This is the most important intellectual hurdle to jump: the illusion that somewhere, there is a solution attached to every problem. The other hurdle, which we shall also encounter in this book, is the intellectual compulsion to think in terms of alternatives, of one thing excluding another: which is the proper finale for Beethoven's Op. 130? The fugue? The second finale? As if there were only one performance, in which case the question would make sense.

But don't let me go into music just yet. My concentric circles, whichever way you arrange them, require a comprehensive, perva-sive view of the need, if any, to criticize, and so far as its ground-plan is concerned, the book will develop along similar lines to 1975's: music alone last but first – even though there will be extended preliminary skirmishes into the world of music, music criticism, and musicology.

And so, at noon after the first, beautifully sunny morning, I am signing off. I hope for much, but only promise one thing with all the considerable fervour at my disposal: not only will there be no phoniness, but phoniness will be fought all the way, explicitly and implicitly. I am indeed implying that the world in general, and the critical world in particular, is full of phoniness which, on the basis of consensus, has acquired the status of truth and/or reality.

Not to speak of the book world, or any other intellectual world. You only have to step into any of them and you are in phoney-land – and, unless you are an inquisitive child, accept it for what it isn't. Take any preface (except for this one). It's the opposite of a preface: it's written after the book, and dated when it's all over. As a result, my own signing off and dating must needs seem positively bizarre. There is an elementary lesson here which this book will heed all along.

HK

Lanzarote, 26 November 1976, 12.05

Part I

PHONEY PROFESSIONS: THE ELEMENT OF CRITICISM

1 Their Nature

For a year or two at the time of writing, I have been going on about what I call phoney professions – for instance, when Professor Boris Ford interviewed me for his *New Universities Quarterly**(an obvious and obviously deliberate successor to F. R. Leavis' *Scrutiny*, though where Leavis was preoccupied with criticism, Ford is preoccupied with education), or when I addressed an international radio conference (*Rencontres de Tenerife*) in March 1976, on *Music on Radio*, or again in the *Spectator*, where I actually used the title 'Phoney Professions'.† This description has indeed been an experiment throughout. Had I chosen a technical term (say, an eminently sociological concept) for what I meant, I should, no doubt, have been listened to with the greatest respect from the outset. Instead, I picked a colloquial, if not vulgar adjective – a word, at the same time, which described what I was talking about, or at least intimated what I would be talking about, with the greatest precision. But unless you use a remotely phoney term (and how many *termini technici* are there that aren't phoney, especially when used towards describing something as yet undiscovered?), you are not taken seriously, because you are not talking the secret language, delightedly half-understood or misunderstood by eavesdroppers, of the particular society – sociological, psychological, musicological – which has occupied, and defined the borders of, an area of permissible discovery.

Most strongly, needless to add, I felt this reaction of amused incredulity ('Maybe his jokes are coming now, with some grotesque wisdom behind them, or maybe he's just pulling our legs') when I lectured to a sociological seminar at the London School of

*Bristol, summer 1976.
†*Spectator*, 18 September 1976.

Economics in the autumn of 1976, and found it necessary to include a section or two on phoney professions in the context of my talk, which was about 'Individual and Collective Conscience'. But in Tenerife, too, I had to overcome the impression that I was but clowning verbally – and, as will be seen presently,* reactions were highly illuminating once I had overcome it. As a matter of fact, the putting up of such a terminological hurdle – the truest word or phrase instead of the professionally trendiest – is eminently worthwhile, for both the depth of the initial puzzlement at what is, after all, the clearest possible word or phrase and the profundity of the subsequent relief at its actually meaning what it means are a clear measure of the strength of your own case.

What I have never yet expounded, but am going to analyse in our present discussion, is the essential role criticism plays in all phoney professions. The exercise of unfavourable criticism does, in fact, seem to be one of the three essential criteria a profession has to meet in order to prove itself phoney – and once it has met all three of them, there is no risk of it not being phoney.

The first criterion, however, is a general one which the phoney profession shares with many professions and occupations that are not at all phoney. Yet it is a *conditio sine qua non* of successful (and hence noticeable) phoney-ism, for it establishes the context within which bogus activities flower until they reach imposing complexity. The profession in question, that is to say, has to be highly respected, indeed admired, within its civilization, or at least that part of its civilization affected by its phoney activities – which are not, of course, ever recognized to be phoney.

The second and central criterion is, on the contrary, extremely specific: *in order to prove its phoniness beyond reasonable doubt, a profession has to create grave problems which it then fails to solve.*

And the third criterion, which we have anticipated and which is almost equally specific, must assume overriding interest within any investigation into the phenomenon of criticism. (Phenomenon: something of which we don't quite know yet what it is, without wishing to own up to the fact.) All phoney professions, that is, stand or fall with their capacity to criticize somebody or something or both – to criticize both negatively and self-righteously, with moralizing aplomb.

---

*See pp. 49–51.

2 Their Paradigm

An exemplification of my thesis can no longer be delayed: what are these phoney professions, which are they? The reason for my procrastination is, of course, the hope that in the meantime, the reader will have thought of one or two phoney professions himself: there is no nobler task a writer, like an educator, can set himself than to prove himself unnecessary at the earliest possible stage in his submissions. But whether he has thought of a phoney profession with which he has been in painful touch or not, he will now welcome my clarifying prototype, my paradigm of a phoney professional: it lies sufficiently far back in the past not to be within immediate sensing distance of any contemporary conflicts or complexes – not even if the reader should be a phoney professional himself, which, statistically speaking, is bloody likely.

The phoney professional *par excellence* – the first, in fact, which I have been able to find in history – is the then highly-respected medieval witch-pricker. Years of medical studies were the first requirement, after which the post-graduate had to go on a two years' witch-prickers' course. Thereafter, and if he had passed his exams, he was professionally qualified as a specialist – qualified to decide, when he pricked a girl, whether she was a witch or not. I need not detail the problems which this profession created and proceeded not to solve, nor is it necessary to demonstrate that the witch-pricker had a permanent object for the most hostile criticism imaginable – the witch. What is necessary, always, is to consider what didn't happen, but could have happened: it's the only reason for living, and living joyfully for the right things to happen. If, that is to say, there had been a genius witch-pricker capable of independent thought and not psychologically dependent on chronic negative criticism, he would have been in an ideal position, professionally qualified, to discover that there weren't any witches

– even though, in the process, he would have become guilty of
professional misconduct, if not indeed of being possessed by the
devil who, as we may presently recognize, is not, perhaps, the
worst person to be possessed by. Unfortunately, as history has
shown us, there weren't any genius witch-prickers, and thousands
of murdered girls had to suffer for the fact – the victims of
unfavourable criticism based on the safest conceivable consensus.

3 Phoney Musical Professions

(i) The Viola Player

Jumping ahead in history and closing in on the world of music (even though a comprehensive inspection of music criticism is reserved for the later stages of this book), we find a veritable galaxy of phoney professions, especially in modern times: it seems that the later stages of a civilization throw them up with ease. There is, pre-eminently, the viola player. Until the earlyish twentieth century, the profession of viola-playing simply did not exist – nor, let us remind ourselves, did the problems of viola-playing, about which we nowadays talk and read and hear a great deal, without any clear-cut solutions yet having been offered.

Until, and indeed slightly beyond, the first quarter of this century, a good violinist automatically was a viola player at the same time; the fact was not worth mentioning. And a Bach, Haydn, Mozart, Beethoven, Schubert or Mendelssohn played the viola just as well as he played the violin. Recent research (by H. C. Robbins Landon) has elicited the fact that with Johann Tost playing the first fiddle, Haydn and Mozart played the viola parts of all the great Mozart string quintets, alternating between first and second viola from movement to movement; that Mozart played the viola in a quartet led by Carl Ditters von Dittersdorf is, of course, well known; in this ensemble, Haydn played the second violin.

The phoney problem of changing between violin and viola, then – a problem which nowadays prevents most violinists from playing the viola and most viola players from playing the violin – just did not exist, did not strike anybody, until well into our own century, but we regard it as downright insuperable. It is explained by the fact that the distances between the notes are greater on the viola than on the violin. So deluded can we become by phoney professionalism that nobody has stopped to think – to discover this basic fallacy that the difference between the first position and the fifth position on the violin, in terms of the respective distances between the fingers, is greater than the difference between the first position on the violin and the first position on the viola. It follows that if the phoney problem were a real problem, there should be, not only professional viola players, but also professional first-position players and professional fifth-position players.

Every violin player and viola player I have confronted with this non-problem has had to give in, at least theoretically. But the emotional strength of a phoney problem – it wouldn't exist without emotional support that passes all understanding – usually tends to make it, in practice, untouchable, however cordial the theoretical agreement with its destruction. At the same time, there are outstanding personalities, some known, many more unknown, who are capable of submitting to their own reasoning instead of confining it for ever to an isolation ward, lest it might affect their lives – the normal human procedure, and suspect like all compulsory confinement without crime. One such toweringly natural mentality is Ida Haendel's; we might all agree that she is, arguably, the greatest woman fiddler alive and playing. Now, I put my case to her about the phoniness of the division between violin-playing and viola-playing – in the same terms as I have expounded it here, if in somewhat greater technical detail. There was silence indicative of theoretical agreement, into which I tried to burst practically: 'Well then, if you were prepared to be realistic, you would accept a suggestion I am now going to make with artistic enthusiasm. Go home, get yourself both Mozart's Sinfonia Concertante for violin and viola and indeed an instrument, and start practising at your ripe age: I guarantee that you'll have the alto clef in your mind and fingers within forty-eight hours – because I know that all the stories about the difficulties of learning the clef come from people who have never tried to learn it. If you agree, I'll arrange a concert for the BBC in which you will, for the first time, appear as a viola player, as well as playing a violin concerto (so as to show that the problems of changing over are phoney), and the violinist in the Concertante will be an artist of your choice.' 'I'd rather discuss him or her with you.' We agreed on Sylvia Rosenberg. 'But I have never as much as touched a viola in my life.' 'So what? What's that supposed to mean?' 'All right, I'll do it.' Pause. 'In fact, I'm already beginning to look forward to it.' At the time of writing, the concert is in its planning stages. When it takes place, it will lend the most powerful support to my theory of phoniness.*

Meanwhile, the critical element in the professional viola player's attitude towards the violin, and in the fiddler's towards the viola, deserves as much attention as the witch-pricker's unconditionally critical attitude towards the potential witch – for the simple reason that they are both about nothing. The viola players would happily turn to the violin (and vice versa) if it were not the 'wrong' instrument from his technical point of view, if its fingerboard did not harbour mortal dangers for his left hand, whose purity might be soiled for ever after – the purity of his intonation, that is. He does not notice that if there are any dangers inherent in the variability of distances between the fingers, he can find the selfsame dangers on his own instrument, without having to change it.

The witch-pricker, likewise, would happily embrace the girl who, when pricked, was able to supply a negative, clinical basis for his bill of health, whereas a proven witch would have soiled his purity for ever after. He did not notice that if there were any dangers inherent in the variability of the human soul and the differences between souls, he could find the selfsame dangers in his own mind as well as in the non-witch's, without having to devote his life to finding witches.

(ii) The Opera Producer

Another phoney profession created by our own time is that of the opera producer who, like the viola player, did not exist in the nineteenth century – nor did the problems of opera production, to whose study the budding opera producer devotes at least as much time as the witch-pricker did to his specialization; in fact, we continually talk (and write) about the problems which the opera producer has created for us, and of which the music lover and opera lover of the eighteenth and nineteenth centuries was blissfully ignorant.

What is even more striking is that the greatest opera productions of which the history of the genre seems to know, and of which we do possess eyewitness accounts, i.e. those of Gustav Mahler at

---

*(The concert never took place. Ed.)

Vienna's Imperial Court Opera, were achieved by a 'mere' theatre musician (and, between ourselves, a sheer musician), to wit, Mahler himself. He had a stage manager at his disposal, to be sure, who looked after the technical side of the dramatic realization, but the basic production ideas, which included décor as well as all considerations about where and how singers ought to, and ought not to move, were decidedly Mahler's own. It was, demonstrably, only after the opera producer had appeared upon the horizon that the world first heard about the intractable problem of opera production, and we, especially we musicians with our inside knowledge of what is going on behind the scenes of an opera house, have never heard the end of it. Without exception, whenever an outstanding conductor prepares an opera, you will find him in profound conflict with an allegedly 'outstanding' opera producer, although this conflict is invariably glossed over in public. It is a mathematical law that the greater the conductor, the greater the conflict: Wilhelm Furtwängler provided extreme evidence. Nor indeed is there any conceivable aesthetic justification for the opera producer functioning as an independent boss, on the same level as the conductor.

When I said, in the Preface, that I was not an opera fan, I should perhaps have added, for those unwilling to understand, that an opera in which the music was not the boss – mere masterly music (say, Wolf-Ferrari's) included, not only great music (and Mozart's *La finta giardiniera* is neither masterly nor great) – did not seem to me to have much of a strictly artistic *raison d'être*; it turns art into a game: what do you want to sing for on a stage if not for the sake of the music? I prefer other games, as unrelated to art as possible, and hence as honest as possible about their nature. Now, if it is accepted that in legitimate opera, the music must needs rule the libretto, being stimulated by it without surrendering to it, it follows that in performance, the conductor has to rule the stage events: anything happening on the stage that contradicts the music, any visual rhythm which is not dominated by musical events, by their own structure, is as helpful as, say, out-of-tune singing.

Yet it is, on the contrary, with his critical attitude towards the conductor, more or less overt, that the opera producer stands or falls, and he knows it: if the constant implication were not that so far as the stage was concerned, the conductor didn't know what he was talking about, or wouldn't if one let him talk, the opera producer would find himself without a job overnight; after all, he had been jobless for centuries, an as yet silent critic of what was happening on the stage, without anybody else noticing anything amiss, whereas now that he has introduced us to the problems of production, plenty of us notice plenty amiss all the time, and many reviews of opera, especially the most professional, have come to concentrate on its phoney aspect, i.e. the production, as if the primary question (though of course not the only one) were not what it all sounded like when you looked the other way – or inward, where, for a developed and imaginative musician, an outstanding production is always available, especially if he knows the composer's stage directions. For they always are the composer's, it will be remembered, not, in their final form, the librettist's.

To end this section on a personal note, but still in an attempt to stimulate reassessment of the role of the theatre in opera, I may perhaps be permitted to add that, composer-librettists apart, I am one of the few musicians, if not indeed the only one, who has actually written a libretto (apart from translating quite a few) – for Benjamin Frankel's *Marching Song* (after John Whiting's play) which, at the time of writing, is still awaiting its first performance.* I thus have first-hand experience of the librettist's function – and the musician in me overpowered the conceptualist with ease, if any overpowering was needed: throughout, the overriding demands of the music – unwritten, half-written, or indeed written (in which case the words had to be fitted in) – were self-evident and spontaneously uppermost in my artistic conscience, and whenever the word or the dramatic action threatened to claim the slightest degree of self-sufficiency, it was instinctively recognized as a mere nuisance.

(iii) The Conductor

Though it is a few pages ago, the reader will, unfortunately, remember that I have been rash enough to talk about great

---

*The composer's last work, it was taken on by the English National Opera, but the production was dropped owing to the financial difficulties in which it would have involved the company.

(The BBC broadcast a studio recording of *Marching Song* on Radio 3 on 3 October 1983. The author subsequently wrote a second libretto, this time for an opera by the Israeli composer Josef Tal, entitled *Der Turm*; performances are planned at the Theater des Westens, Berlin, on 19 and 20 September 1987. Ed.)

conductors. I shouldn't have done: it was intellectual shorthand, used in order not to be deflected from my conclusion about the phoniness of the opera producer, in order not to allow the argument to become cumbersome. For the truth is that there is no such thing as a great conductor, just as there was no such thing as a great witch-pricker: conducting itself is a phoney profession too, which has created the lamentable problem of orchestral playing – an insoluble problem, as every orchestral player knows (including myself, at an infantile stage). There have, of course, been very great musicians amongst conductors; the greatest, in my lifetime, was Furtwängler, and possibly the greatest of all times was Mahler, significantly enough not just, or even mainly, a conductor.

Now, there was no problem of orchestral playing when the professional conductor as we know him did not yet exist, and let us not forget that while older than the viola player or the opera producer, he is not nearly as old as is most of the music of which he has now taken charge – and which, owing to the problems he has created, cannot possibly be done without him. However, before he came in and went about his business of stupefying the orchestra and thus making it dependent upon him, orchestral musicians were intelligent enough, had to be, to cope with the problems of ensemble playing and choral playing (i.e. *tutti* playing, the playing of a part with more than one instrument to it). The conductor's existence is, essentially, superfluous, and you have to attain a high degree of musical stupidity in order to find watching the beat, or the conductor's inane face for that matter, easier for the purpose of knowing when and how to play than simply listening to the music. But such established, collective stupidity is the conductor's very lifeblood, and it must be admitted that his attempts to maintain it at a steady level in order to justify his existence, his quick and skilful suppression of any sign of intelligence, let alone independent thought, have proved brilliantly successful.

At the same time, he has not bargained for what is, no doubt, the gravest side of the unsolvable problem of orchestral playing he has created single-handed: how does one make an orchestral player like his work? The conductor would dearly like to solve that one if he could. Since he can't, he habitually denies the problem to himself and, if challenged, to others. It is a pity that you never see him with the orchestra during an interval in rehearsal: the chances are that in that situation, he could pick up more reality from the players than they can ever pick up from him. Above all, he would notice that if, in such an interval, you talk about music in any but the most sneering terms, your verbal conduct runs the gravest risk of being considered unprofessional; the love of music is confined to amateur orchestras, even though you may not be able to hear it.

I submit as a verifiable fact that there is not a single musical orchestral player in the world who would not dearly love to get out of the orchestra if he could: those who can, invariably do. Without my help, the informed reader will easily recall a distinguished list of names which even includes some of our most outstanding leaders, even though the leader's musical position in the orchestra is relatively privileged: Hugh Maguire, Manoug Parikian, Erich Gruenberg ... I have no knowledge of the financial circumstances of these gentlemen, but I know about orchestral salaries and soloistic or chamber-musical freelance earnings, and I would not be surprised if such departures from orchestras usually entailed, at least temporarily, a marked drop in the individual's and his family's living standards.

Under the influence of the conductor, orchestral playing has, in short, become an unmusical occupation. The disintegration of the permanent large symphony orchestra, which we are currently witnessing, is the latest sign of a crisis which was produced by one of the most powerful phoney professions in the musical world.

The conductor's inevitable attitude of criticism towards the orchestral player springs from the absolute need for him to know better: either he can make himself, the orchestral player, and the public believe that he knows better, or else there is no place for his profession as it stands, for him where he stands. Let us face the brutal truth: either he is, at every given moment, more musical, more intelligent, more knowledgeable than every single orchestral player he conducts, or else he has no artistic right to overrule him where there is a difference of opinion. In practice, the only way out of this unsolvable situation is constantly to degrade the player by more or less loving criticism, faking a spot of consultation in between: the enthusiasm with which members of the public attend rehearsals in order to witness this – often quite unmusical – degradation, this specific proof of conducting mastery (as if, technically, there were anything to master!) is a measure of the need for criticism by proxy, with which we shall have to concern ourselves more closely at a later stage.★ For the moment, we note that the conductor has this in common with his unconfessed arch-enemy, the opera producer – that he has to know better if he wants to survive: the producer has to know better than the conductor, and the conductor has to know better than any orchestral player – even though this player may be – let us dive into the safe past – Arnold Rosé, Mahler's brother-in-law and the historic quartet leader who, at the same time, led the Vienna Court Orchestra, later the Vienna Philharmonic Orchestra, from his late teens until his mid-sixties – until, that is, he was removed by the Nazis: in the infamous history of orchestral playing, no great musician had ever played under so many mediocrities who knew better (as well as one or two great musicians, such as Mahler himself and Furtwängler – whose approach to their job was strikingly similar, according to those who played under them: Arnold Rosé, his cellist Friedrich Bux-baum, and another cellist who was a substantial composer at the same time, Franz Schmidt).

The reader may well ask: if my reasoning is realistic, how was it possible for Rosé to stay in the orchestra for a span of two genera-tions? Franz Schmidt left as soon as he could, while Friedrich Buxbaum, the lesser musician, stayed on, perhaps because Rosé did. I feel like reacting to this question as John Cage did when he had to face an uncomfortable rhetorical question at the end of one of his lectures: 'That's a good question. Next question!' The truth is that Rosé's was an extraordinarily tough personality – most unusual for a singularly sensitive artist.† Life was, of course, made easier by the circumstance that he probably was the most respected orchestral leader that ever was – but nevertheless, as the leader of a world famous quartet and the holder of an elevated teaching post, who, moreover, could ask for private lessons what he liked (one of his pupils taught me as a child), he could have well afforded to turn his back on the tiresome double task of playing at the State Opera

---

★See pp. 124ff.

†As a child, I still heard him on numerous occasions – in all three capacities, i.e. as a leader, quartet leader, and indeed as a soloist: relevantly to our discussion, I might record that in a concert in which Bronislaw Huberman featured as a soloist, Rosé got up from his leader's desk, exchanged his violin for a viola, and played Mozart's Concertante with the virtuoso – the profoundest and most tone-conscious performance I ever heard, and by tone-conscious, I mean the awareness of the difference in tonal character between the violin and the viola.

and in the Philharmonic Orchestra's symphony concerts.

But the toughness of his character actually seemed to make him enjoy superficial, if not pretended, subordination – beyond which he didn't give way an inch: psychologically speaking, within himself, he made a fool of people who, as a matter of professional (read: phoney) expertise, reduced his role to that of a fool. It was indeed fascinating to observe how this eminently natural toughness radiated in the most diverse directions, one of them truly unexpected: though he played a valuable Italian instrument, he chose strings of such extraordinary thickness for it that he wellnigh obliterated its character. His own characteristic (noble and chaste) tone was there, to be sure, but in the circumstances, he could just as easily have produced it on a common or garden instrument.

Compared to the 'normal' violinist's preoccupation with, and narcissistic love of his own instrument, if it is his chosen one, Rosé's attitude towards the instrument or instruments he elected to play was so tough that it seemed downright negligent to the 'normal', conventional observer. In his early twenties, as perhaps the most youthful leader the Vienna Philharmonic ever had, he played a cheap instrument which even he had to admit was not altogether adequate. Now, a proper, respectable violinist needs weeks to get used to an instrument, and to adjust it to his own personality, to 'play it in'. Rosé, on the other hand, would drop in on his favourite violin-maker of an early morning: 'Do you happen to have a good Italian instrument around which I could borrow for a day? I've got a big solo at the opera tonight!' It is, I suggest, in view of this amazing toughness of his, which I have never seen recur in an artist of remotely comparable stature, that Arnold Rosé can be fitted into the context of my argument, without any friction remaining.

(Interlude) A Musician's Support

At the same time, our train of thought has to be functionally interrupted at this very stage in order to yield to a thematic episode of considerable proportions – which, I fondly hope, will assume the role of a central episode in a developed – indeed developmental – sonata rondo. When people introduce new thoughts and feel proportionately insecure and defensive – even the strongest, like Freud or Schoenberg, found it difficult to escape this (as I would call it) intellectual war neurosis – they are usually all the gladder to be able to cite the occasional 'authority' in their support, however little they may think of the work of that authority when it doesn't confirm their own. Sensibly or not, I have always reacted against this successful cry for help on – dare I say it? – moral grounds: you either have discovered something or you haven't, and the fact that an authority, or another authority, also thinks that twice two makes four doesn't make your case any stronger – for the clear reason that if your case were that twice two made four and a half, and if you found an 'authority' to support you, that wouldn't make your case any stronger either.

However, there are authorities and authorities. There are what we might describe as the automatically useful authorities – the people who have successfully researched in the same field as you have, leading psychologists if you are a psychologist, leading musicologists if you are a musicologist and, needless to add, leading opera producers if you are an opera producer. There is no doubt that if a witch-pricker had discovered a new way of finding or defining a witch, he'd have been only too delighted if he had been able to quote authoritative witch-pricking sources that could be taken to confirm, or at least foreshadow, his daring conclusions. In short, these are the authorities who are supposed to know, though whether they know or not is another question: sometimes they do, and sometimes they don't.

On the other hand, there are the authorities, rarely so called, who are right inside the situation into which you are researching, and who, at the same time, are minds of such power and penetration that the situation and what it means or might mean is right inside them. They are the people with inner authority, immediately recognizable to those who have inner authority themselves – the people who *know*, though whether they are supposed to know is another question: sometimes they are, and usually they aren't.

I am fortunate enough to be able to remind the reader that the inner authority whose support I am about to enlist is indeed supposed to know; the likely reader of the present book, at any rate, even if he strongly objects to my thesis about phoney professions, will happily accept that my witness should know.

After I had written my piece about 'Phoney Professions' for the *Spectator*,★ and aware that Benjamin Britten's days were numbered,

★See p. 13.

while sensing that he – in spite, or because of having been an exclusive viola player as well as an outstanding conductor and a long-standing collaborator of leading opera producers – would understand my thesis both more comprehensively and more specifically than any prospective reader I knew, I decided, against my stern practice never to invite anybody (except my closest friends and any direct addressees) to read anything I had written, to send him a copy of the essay upon publication – for reasons which I stated in an accompanying note, i.e. that I would value his opinion, which was habitually frank. What I hoped but did not say was that he would see beyond the jokes, seriously as I meant them – that whatever was humorous about the piece was merely designed to throw the gravity of my case into readable relief, and to let the sun shine into damp and, normally, shady corners.

Some time elapsed. Meanwhile, I had been told of his latest condition, and had begun to reproach myself with having bothered him, who now devoted his few strong daily hours exclusively to composition, with a problem which could not possibly compare with any compositional problem that was engaging his mind – when his reply arrived. Dated 27 October 1976, it must have been one of the last, if not the last letter he wrote, or rather dictated: writing with his paralysed right hand was difficult, though one correction and the signature had been handwritten, while the letter itself was typed. I received it with joy, but without surprise; I had not envisaged the possibility that he would disagree:

Dear Hans,

Sorry not to acknowledge 'Phoney professions' before this, but life has not been simple. Three cheers for it,* say I! I have long talked on these lines about conductors and producers and I sincerely hope that your wise words will have some effect. The idea [of] the viola and violin players is a new one to me, but very good. Why do they not learn from the clarinet players?

Yours ever,
Ben.

Five points emerge, the last perhaps the most important in our context. First, the phrase, 'your wise words' had been typed as

---

*A reference, no doubt, to *Albert Herring* (Act II, Scene i), on which I had written the first analysis.

'your witty words'; Britten deleted 'witty' and inserted the word 'wise' above it. I have meanwhile ascertained that the shorthand outline of 'wise' cannot possibly be mistaken for that of 'witty': Britten must have changed his mind. That really gratified me: if I am dismayed about anything in the effect of my writings, it is not mere incomprehension or hostility, but the fact that my jokes often seem successfully to hide the deeper meaning, if any. I loathe nothing more than the solemn delivery of wisdom, its imposition on other people – so whenever I suspect that a little bit of wisdom may have come my way, humorous communication of it becomes an irresistible temptation. That Britten had easily seen through me, as he and everybody else had been intended to, showed my method to be not altogether invalid.

Secondly, it is indeed charming to note Britten's frank naïvety, characteristically a great man's: the one idea that was 'a new one' to him was the phoniness of Britten the viola player: he should have been a violinist too! Thirdly, the excellent idea that viola players and violinists should learn from clarinettists is, shockingly, a new one to me in my turn: I was too preoccupied with the palpable idiocy of the separation between the instruments, too deeply involved in its history and results, to spare a thought for possible positive counter-examples – of non-separation.

Fourthly, one is once again reminded that discoveries, insights, are but rarely individual; what, to begin with, is individual is their public disclosure – which is ineluctably tactless because it goes against established convention. Maybe it is just because one reminds people of their own, barely repressed insights that the weaker among them tend to react against one's disclosures with such passionate hostility. Freud's discoveries of the unconscious and repression, of infantile sexuality, and the Oedipus complex, are, of course, gigantic examples, the very mention of which may seem grotesquely immodest in the present context – but extreme examples have always been helpful in making a piece of truth visible to the naked eye. Another example, hardly less extreme but nonetheless totally, and significantly, unrecognized for what it signifies, is Hans Pfitzner's violent hostility, publicly recorded in the most tedious detail, to Schoenberg's atonal revolution. Down the decades, critics have devoted thousands and thousands of words to the ensuing controversy with Alban Berg, but not a single critic has drawn attention to the fact – immeasurably more interesting both musically and psychologically – that in his masterly opera, *Palestrina*, Pfitzner occasionally moves right into the no-man's-land between tonality and atonality, if not indeed into momentarily atonal harmonic structures altogether: his guilt feelings about what his genius made him express against his theoretical will must have been as intense as they were unconscious.

(iv) The Music Critic

Lastly, since I have ventured to mention, not merely criticism, but actual music critics at this early stage, I may as well confess, most thematically – returning to the principal sections of my movement, in fact – that the remaining phoney professionals I listed in my *Spectator* piece were critics, musicologists, and so-called 'professional broadcasters'. The fact that the greatest – or the only great? – British composer since Elgar accepted, without hesitation or reservation, the phoniness of music criticism as a profession cannot, I suggest, be ignored by the reader, including the critic-reader who, of necessity, will be the only reader reacting to this book in public print. I would go so far as to say that the phoniness of professional music criticism, if not of art criticism generally, would have been exposed a long time ago, publicly and definitively, if the potential exposers had not been aware, or had not thought they were aware, that sociologically speaking, they just had no chance: their books would have been reviewed by critics, not by composers and performers – and that, they wrongly felt, would have been that. They felt it wrongly because they wrongly felt that critics were monsters. By no means: I have learnt, first painfully, then joyfully, that as people, critics are no worse than you and I; at times (rarely, of course, don't worry), they are, as people, considerably better than you and I.

If and when they are, they are going to react to this book, not enthusiastically, of course, but emotionfully as well as thoughtfully – and any reaction that is genuinely emotionful does not leave conflicting emotions out of account. What I am suggesting is that to one or the other critic, I hope to demonstrate, at least intermittently, the validity of his own discoveries, the way Freud demonstrated the validity of ours to us, or Schoenberg and Berg the validity of Pfitzner's to Pfitzner, not to speak of my addressing Britten about his discoveries. The rest will be the critic's problem, not mine – if, that is to say, what I submit is true. For there is one consoling thing about the truth, even when it is not recognized: it can wait, whereas the false or semi-false – opportunism – can't.

Viewed outside this inevitable confrontation between myself and the music critics, however, criticism could be argued to be the most self-evident phoney profession since witch-pricking, even though no innocents are killed in the process – not quite. About the status the profession enjoys in our civilization there need not be much argument, even though much can be said about it: virtually the only people who despise the profession are considerable artists. Mediocre artists tend to regard it with greater favour, partly because they are prepared to take the problems the critic creates – such as, in the music of our time, memorability – for real, and partly because they use, or try to use, or hope to use, the critic as their publicity agent, even if it means deleting any reservations he has about their art in order to be able to print the rest of his verdict in their brochures, on their book flaps, on theatre posters, etc. He himself minds, of course, but he does not – unless he is as outstanding amongst critics as Furtwängler was amongst conductors – mind too much, because he likes being printed and reprinted; he is, in short, providing the artist with the publicity the artist provides him with.

This, of course, is only true on a lowish level, but you would be surprised how many lowish levels there are; the rare levels are only the lowest and the high. In any case, by society as a whole, the critic is highly esteemed because, once again, it is his job, his *raison d'être*, to know better – not better than the reader in the first place, but better than someone else, than whom the reader also knows better as soon as he has read the critic; and since this someone else is an artist who, as psychological discoverer presuming above the ordinary mortal's station, will always arouse ambivalence in proportion to the depth of his discoveries, there will always be a desire, latent at least, to degrade the artist, either socially and/or as a madman, and the critic is the main, deeply valued instrument of all such degradation. What is more, he praises too, and thus serves society's uncomfortable ambivalence all-embracingly, and therefore comfortably.

Because his role is one of central psychological significance (as distinct from importance) for all parties concerned, the problems which the critic creates without solving them have always been underrated, if they have been recognized at all. Primarily, of course, he creates problems for the artist: professing to have discovered artistic deficiencies, he will, as often as not, invent them and thus saddle the artist with the experience of having been libelled without having any chance of redress – a profound human problem if ever there was one. As a young man, I consistently defended Schoenberg's music against the critics. Then I was the odd man out, whereas nowadays what I suggested is accepted as aesthetic fact, almost commonplace fact. But at the time, the composer (who didn't know me) sent me, out of gratitude, first his just-published book *Style and Idea* with a dedication, and then some idiotic criticism of his twelve-tone music with the pathetic request to invalidate it.* As a youngster, I found it wellnigh incomprehensible that Schoenberg should bother; meanwhile, I have learnt that there are but few artists who are as tough *vis-à-vis* the insoluble problems which the phoney professions create for them as Arnold Rosé was. The Law and Morality are, naturally enough, brothers-in-law rather than natural brothers: if Schoenberg had been accused, in public, of having stolen the afore-mentioned loaf of bread, he would have been far less hurt than he was by the hostile criticisms of his work; he would have wasted far less time and psychological energy on overcoming the insult, in addition to which he could have conducted a successful libel or slander action, which would have reduced the total amount of time and energy wasted still further.

As it was, the very critics who tried their efficient best to make him feel persecuted (and he would have had to be a halfwit for such feelings not to arise) proceeded to accuse him of paranoia – another unsolvable problem they had created with masterly skill. It is quite true that at least from the atonal revolution onwards, his personality showed distinct paranoid traits, but the question remains which came first, the boiled, or rather boiling chicken† or the rotten egg. It has to be added that I am choosing Schoenberg, once

---

*I subsequently incorporated it in my extended essay, 'Schoenberg and the Men of the Press', *Music Survey*, London, March 1951. A facsimile of his letter was reproduced in *Music Survey*, June 1952.
†In May 1947, in response to being awarded a grant of $1,000 by the National Institute of Arts and Letters, New York, Schoenberg recorded a speech of thanks in which he described the subjective experience of the atonal revolution: 'I had the feeling as if I had fallen into an ocean of boiling water.'

again, as an extreme example; my first-hand knowledge of the emotional problems which critics have created for great and considerable artists, both composers and performers, could easily fill a long, boring, and depressing book. The logical question with its emotional consequences is simple: it is a question of diametrically opposed, alternative situations producing the selfsame result. Either, that is, the critic is wrong, in which case there would have to be something wrong with the artist if he did not feel that he has been damaged, or rather, that his work has – whence he is unhappy. Or the critic is right, in which case the artist will, consciously or unconsciously, sense the fact and feel publicly exposed, all the more so since valid negative criticisms are not usually placed in perspective by the critic – linked to equally valid positive criticisms of the work or performance in question, which would have to be expressed with equal fervour. Unfortunately, negative fervour comes more easily, more articulately, than positive fervour – especially on lowish levels of criticism. And so the artist is unhappy again, because the critic is right – just as unhappy as he would be if the critic were wrong.

It has often been said, above all by critics, of course, that every artist worth his salt ought to be able to 'take it'. This is the morality of the gutter – the belief in the survival of the fittest in any situation, regardless of the purpose for which fitness is, or should be, desirable. Speaking as one who has proved himself able to take hostile public criticism all his life without having his chronic good mood disturbed, I cannot be suspected of special pleading when I suggest that no attempt has ever been made to show why the artist should be able 'take it'. His only ascertainable duty is to express what he has to express as clearly and as briefly as possible, not to say anything that has been said before, nor anything that isn't true of the human mind, as distinct from merely his own. This is the task for which he has to be fit, indeed fittest, and if he accomplishes it more easily when he is left in peace, so be it; most of us accomplish most things more easily when we are left in peace. The only conceivable argument in favour of the substantial artist being able to withstand attacks is fallacious: it is the history of genius, and genius has indeed proved itself capable not only of taking any kind of adversity, but of turning it into something fruitful. Beethoven's deafness is the clearest possible extreme example: it is arguable that without it, he could not have achieved the total independence of contemporary sound ideals which his last-period works evince, particularly the five late string quartets and the Grand Fugue. But is it going to be said, therefore, that every composer worth his salt ought to be able to take deafness? What Beethoven did with it happened on the plane of supreme genius – genius of an order of which this total transmutation of the worst possible adversity was indeed a measure.

Smetana's genius, too, was able to 'take it', but on a much lower level – despite the gripping high harmonic E which, at the end of his First String Quartet, announces his approaching deafness. But his slightly fragmentary Second Quartet, though far too little known, cannot, of course, compare with the masterly first: deafness had not produced the same effect as in the case of Beethoven. And while the very bittiness of this work, ultimately due, no doubt, to the composer's unhappiness about his physical state, prophetically forehears the unhappiness of music as a whole which was to dominate the twentieth century, it is evident from the audible difficulties Smetana encountered in composing it that without his genius (but still plenty of talent), he would not, creatively, have survived his deafness at all. How do we know how many talents did not survive their critics? I know quite a few who only just survived them – sometimes with my help as a teacher.

So much for the primary problems which criticism creates without solving them, without making any attempt to solve them – without, in most cases, being aware of them, though unconscious awareness can often be noted in all conscience, covered as it is by frantic denial whenever you are fool enough to raise the subject. The secondary problems which the critic creates are, likewise, beyond his conscious reach – if he is a typical, i.e. 'thoroughly professional' critic anyway. If the primary problems are created for the artist, with the public, inevitably, being the co-sufferer (for it is of the nature of art that the artist cannot suffer alone), the secondary problems are created for the public, with the artist being the co-sufferer (for it is of the nature of art that the quality of perception, of listening in the case of music, affects the artist). The only reason why I describe the latter problems as secondary is that they concern the process of getting it across (communication), more than the process of getting it out (creation).

In the autumn of 1976, in a valuable symposium on music

criticism organized by McMaster University, Canada, in which I was, as usual, the only outspoken dissident from a number of majority verdicts more or less glibly arrived at, the one conclusion on which, eventually, everybody seemed to agree was that the critic was, or should be, a bridge between the composer and the listener, a bridge all the more necessary at a time when there was an inevitable cleft, if not an abyss, between the contemporary composer and his potential audience.

Like most abstract propositions of, essentially, a moralistic or educational nature, this one sounds good, unproblematic, so long as you don't face it with honest, concrete thought – and with empirical thought into the bargain. To revert to my favourite and, by now, historic example of the Music Critic of *The Times* ruling, at a crucial stage in the history of listening, that Schoenberg was not a composer at all: what sort of bridge was that? If anything, he widened the gulf abysmally – nor, of course, did a man of his official authority remain alone for long. What makes this example – once again an extreme case, for not every critic, not even every 'authority', evinced quite that degree of musical inanity at the time – so sadly amusing is that we now know that if there was one composer in this century who needed the bridge above all others, and the understanding of whose music was a precondition for the understanding of the music of our time, it was Schoenberg. Most of the critical bridges that have, in fact, been built are bridges across nothing – fly-overs which may make the journey faster, but proportionately less perceptive; and since, in music, it is not merely better to travel than to arrive, but all arrival is in fact a dead end, an illusion, the countless critical bridges from and to the classics and romantics have concealed more than they have disclosed.

The first requirement for a successful bridge is, in fact, suspension of judgement, of evaluation, whereas the first thing criticism does and is expected to do in the face of new music is to evaluate: little would be left of criticism if evaluation did not take place, whence the classics and romantics don't escape reassessments either. Evaluation is the most effective defence the human mind has devised against what it feels to be a threat, and all new art is felt to be a threat if it is good – new and true – enough.

What criticism has done down the ages, then, is exactly the opposite of bridge-building. My extreme example serves: consistently, criticism has put obstacles in the way of understanding, has

even destroyed bridges laboriously built by the public, the
recipients of art themselves; it is here that the secondary problems
lie which criticism has created. Nor is it only the 'advanced' type of
music which tends to fall victim to the critic's help; decades ago, it
was not only the music of Schoenberg or Webern whose understanding was postponed at the instructions of the critical faculty. If
Schoenberg was too advanced, Britten was too conservative, and
with one or two exceptions (Desmond Shawe-Taylor outstanding
amongst them), the critics consistently slowed down the understanding of his music by 'proving' it to be facile, superficially
brilliant and virtuosic, and hence suspect. Nor was Schoenberg
alone in not being forgiven for not repeating himself (i.e. his tonal
music): for many years, nothing Britten wrote could hope to be as
good as *Peter Grimes* – though that wasn't considered all that good
when it first appeared upon the scene; after all, it didn't repeat any
previous achievement of his either. I have personal knowledge of
how deeply such criticisms affected the composer – not musically,
of course, but humanly.

As I write on a normally secluded beach of this little Canary
Island, the idyllic peace is interrupted by a noisy film crew, who
seem to be taking ages to decide what to film, how to film it, and
precisely why. The director, an American all of whose intellect
seems to be residing in his beard, is holding forth on the story and
how it has to be expressed. My wife and I are mildly interested in
what the whole thing is about – whether the expenditure in money
and energy (the big crew has been staying at our hotel for the past
few days, and drinking heavily) bears any relation to the artistic
aim, if any. Who knows, a novel type of film of rich complexity
might be in the making, and we might be granted the opportunity
to be in on the opening stages. However, since I am heavily
preoccupied with the present book, my interest, though alive, is
still milder than my wife's, so she investigates, not I.

It is an unbearable pity that I cannot pose the question of the
precise nature of this picture, sorry, movie, in the form of a quiz to
the reader – and that my wife, who likes quizzes, was too excited
by her discovery to pose the quiz to me: the film was going to be a
commercial for 7-Up. After our excitement had died down and our
observations, not easily printable, about the state of our civilization
had been exchanged, I could not help absorbing the little trauma
into the context of my current cogitations: when all is filmed and

nothing done, what causes more harm, what is a more deadening waste of time and effort – the ten-or-so seconds of the finished product, the 7-Up film, or the hundred-or-so bars which, at the very least, distinguished critics prevented a Schoenberg or Britten from writing because a good deal of energy had to be devoted to overcoming distress? Or again, what about the ten-or-so years which, at the very least, critical obstacle-building inserted between a work's possible understanding and its actual understanding?

In recent years, to be sure, much obstacle-building has been replaced by the building of flimsy bridges – amounting to a new set of problems which the profession of criticism has created. Impressed, that is to say, by the total failure of their forefathers to catch up with new developments and recognize new major talent, not to speak of the genius of a Schoenberg or Britten (or Gershwin, for that matter), the latest generation of music critics, and to some extent of critics of the other arts, has decided to rush into positive evaluation without the slightest understanding – just to be on the safe side. Pseudo-bridges are being built now, cardboard bridges that give themselves the appearance of concrete – but when you step on them, they and you crash into the abyss. The new method of positive incomprehension has even affected the older critics who, para-doxically, *are now far more tolerant towards the latest nonsense than they were towards the latest sense twenty years ago*. The result remains the same: positive incomprehension is as much of an obstacle, as much of a problem for the recipient of art to whom it is addressed, as negative incomprehension – nor does it delight the creator's heart any more, apart from the smallest creative hearts, which usually do not encounter much incomprehension anyway.

If genuine, musical bridge-building is necessary and possible at all – curious conjunction of adjectives? – it is the job of analysis, not of criticism. It may be necessary and not possible – which would be an intellectual tragedy. It may be possible and not necessary, which would be an intellectual luxury, not to say superfluity. In any case, the question of the difference between criticism and analysis, and between description and either, will have to wait until we confine ourselves to music and its criticism.★

★See Part III, Section 2, pp. 134ff.

(v) The Musicologist

Meanwhile, it cannot possibly be said that our next, long-awaited phoney profession, that of musicology, is about music alone; in fact, when you read, or listen to, some of the products of musicological research and reconstruction, you may be forgiven for wondering whether it is about music at all – and the situation is not always improved, rendered more musical, if it is the musicologists themselves who do the actual playing of the music. Like viola-playing, conducting and criticism, the profession of musicology has indeed been able to accommodate outstanding musicians in its ranks – who, however (again like their counterparts in the other phoney professions) have not succeeded in turning their own discipline into a less phoney profession. Musicology is, perhaps, the most awe-inspiring profession in the musical world, and amongst respectable ignoramuses the most respected, if not the most loved or admired. Like criticism, however, it enjoys scant respect amongst practising musicians, even though nowadays – in an era which is becoming ever more musicologically orientated – they will only confess in private to their contempt for the discipline and its practitioners. But the reason for their ungrateful attitude towards this relatively new science, or pseudo-science, which is supposed to help them, is not, I am afraid, its phoniness: they haven't discovered that yet, although I am confident that they will be delighted to hear about it.

No, the reason why they heartily dislike musicology is that they abhor most individual musicologists they know from the bottom of their gall-bladders; and the very potent reason why they hate these musicologists is that on closer acquaintance, they turn out to be rather unmusical. If you are musical, you are likely to do something more musical than musicology.

You are likely to, but not bound to. One towering musicality amongst living musicologists, perhaps *the* most musical and, significantly enough, a leading light in, and far beyond his profession, is H. C. Robbins Landon; and it was he who cordially agreed with me some years ago when I wrote in a musicological journal that the fancy term of 'musicology', suggesting a science where there wasn't any,* was totally unnecessary to say the least; there was musical

---

*Originally, it is, in fact, a translation of the German *Musikwissenschaft* (literally, 'the science of music'), which was introduced by Hugo Riemann, much to the distress of leading Austro-German musicians, Franz Schmidt amongst them.

history, I said, there was textual criticism, and there was research into past practices of performance, but there wasn't anything else – so why call what there was musicology?

That does not mean, of course, that the profession could be acquitted, divested of its phoniness, if it dropped its name. It's not what they are called, it's what they do – though what they call themselves does confirm their elemental need for bogus prestige. And once again, we might fruitfully remind ourselves that Benjamin Britten, whose interest in pre-classical music, both as a composer and a performer, has powerfully enriched the music and musical life of the twentieth century without harming a seventeenth-century or eighteenth-century fly (and God knows there are some bluebottles amongst them) – that this very same Benjamin Britten accepted my description of musicology as a phoney profession with enthusiasm (and had done so long before our exchange late in 1976). Especially when preparing his performances of pre-classical music, he was, of course, in detailed contact with the problems which musicologists have created without solving them in anybody's opinion except their own – and, maybe, the opinion of their lackeys, most of them bad or inhibited performers scraping a living – in terms less of money than of self-respect – with performances which, critics tell the bewildered public, it must listen to and enjoy or else.

In particular, I am thinking of Britten's anti-musicological performance of Bach's *St John Passion*. Lest it be thought that I was unduly prejudiced in favour of Britten's approach, let me hasten to add that I thought, rightly or wrongly, that it was one of the worst of the hundreds of performances I had heard of this monument of metaphysical art – but I did not think so for musicological reasons: it was the barely concealed sadism (characteristic of the unconditional pacifist!) replacing transcendental drama that disturbed me – and could be shown to give rise to illogical phrasings which, admittedly, were always clarity itself and as such impressive: give me Britten's wrong phrasings any time instead of Boulez's non-phrasings, or the typical mediocrity's* utility phrasings that might mean anything or nothing, with more than one main accent per phrase to choose from.

---

*Only mediocrities (like Kafka's Gregor Samsa in 'Metamorphosis' or his K. in *The Trial*) and sub-mediocrities are typical. If we describe those who transcend mediocrity as typical of something or other, we try to degrade, de-individualize them.

Pre-eminently, the problems which musicology has created are, of course, those of authenticity. Historical conditions have to be re-established, historical instruments used, historical styles of playing learnt. I am not condemning historical interest and its musical possibilities out of hand; what I am condemning is the slightest disloyalty to the ear, your ear and mine: 'The ear', said Schoenberg in one of the most unexceptionable of his more radical statements, 'is the musician's sole brain.' Whereas some of the musicological endeavours to change our performing practice of old music are as closely linked to spontaneous aural perception and cognition as would be the demand – I am surprised it has not yet been made in musicological quarters – to play Bach by candle-light.

And there's worse. What are, superficially, some of the most plausible musicological requirements, making sense to the ear and the brain – which depend on habit, especially recently established habit with its gratifying revolutionary appearance! – turn out, upon inspection and reflection, to be delusions of authenticity such as could grace any ward of a progressive mental hospital welcoming the victims of newly discovered mental diseases, amongst whom the sufferers from musicological delusions would surely figure prominently. As a shining example, take the musicological reaction, which has by now become well established, against so-called 'romantic'* interpretations of pre-classical (and indeed classical) music – interpretations which, so far as string-playing was concerned, included a generous measure of what musicologists call portamenti and musicians call glissandos and music lovers call scoops or slides. When the musicological reaction set in – in the first third of our century, I suppose – the scoops were out, all of them, and from a scholarly point of view, they have been out, or should have been out, ever since. Old recordings, from the early thirties or earlier, of string virtuosi playing Bach make every decent and decently educated modern ear shudder and smile in turn, so civilized have we become, musicologically speaking.

The problem that musicology had created in this particular area, then, was the presence of undesirable scoops all over the place, and the solution seemed equally clear: if you slide you're sacked. But

---

*When applied to music, I do not understand the concept of romanticism in any case. If, that is to say, there is definable meaning attached to the term at all, music is a romantic art.

how did, and do, the musicologists know that Bach didn't slide about? What is their evidence? The music? To my knowledge which, in this field, is comprehensive, not a single piece of intra-musical evidence has been advanced to support what I – with concrete reason, as will be seen – consider the illusion of pre-classical or classical scooplessness. The sustained musicological reaction to and against 'romanticism' has, in fact, been just as emotional, just as uncontrolled by reason, as the 'romantic' players were supposed to be – except that the musicologists are being emotionally anti-emotional, which psychological condition ties them up in knots: they are no longer capable of inspecting their own beloved historical evidence, or of subjecting Bach's string parts to the kind of textual criticism which might furnish some hard musical evidence towards the solution of the embarrassing question – to slide or not to slide.

In my submission, the solution is, simply, the performing prac-tice before the musicologists came in, well fortified by the twentieth century's anti-romantic explosion whose smoke seems, at last, to be clearing: unfortunately, there is no fire without smoke, which tends to hang in the air long after the fire itself has burnt out.

Here is my own evidence – which I have thrown at every musicologist as well as at every violinist and theorist about string-playing I have come across, always with the same result, to wit, unqualified acceptance of my anti-musicological case. The greatest single revolution in the technique of violin-playing and viola-playing was not *The Art of Violin Playing* by Carl Flesch – though the overpowering influence this utterly unique player-teacher had on the development of violin-playing, at least the western style, is still gravely underestimated; there has, in fact, been no other great player who has been as great and as influential a pedagogue, no other great teacher who has been a front-rank virtuoso at the same time. Yet the revolution he initiated cannot compare to the effect of the introduction of a simple mechanical device, a mechanical aid to violin-playing, to wit, the chin-rest.

Louis Spohr, a great nineteenth-century virtuoso, a small com-poser and, with his quartet, one of the first exponents of Beet-hoven's Op. 18 quartets (with which he went on tour), had a long neck, as contemporary pictures will verify. It was, no doubt, as a result of this physical handicap that he invented the chin-rest – thus changing, overnight, the violinist's possible answers to the question of changing position. Before he had introduced the chin-rest, that is, the instrument had to be held in, and with, the left hand alone; the chin could not take any part in the holding, since it would have slipped off the belly of the violin if it had tried. Came the chin-rest, and the possibility arose of holding the instrument, on the contrary, with the chin alone; by the time Carl Flesch defined the basic principles of violin technique, the sole rule of the chin had become a firm convention, any other holding of the violin (say, the gypsies') strictly non-U – so much so that I personally have only known two outstanding violinists who were able to play the violin without a chin-rest at all: Oskar Adler, in his teens Schoenberg's first (self-taught) teacher and subsequently his lifelong friend, and Norbert Brainin, the leader of the Amadeus Quartet, who has kept his passion for technical unconventionalities and changes of established practice alive throughout his distinguished career.

What, above all, prevents the less extraordinary mortal from playing without a chin-rest is the difficulty of changing position without the instrument being firmly held between chin and collarbone. If such a change is accomplished at all, probably between positions tolerably close to each other, it cannot possibly be effected without glissando – and that goes for the Alders and Brainins and indeed the gypsies too: all chin-rest-less playing must needs incorporate well-audible sliding in its technique of changing position. The fact, then, that the gypsies operate, or used to operate, with plenty of slides is not just due to their being naughty and emotional and natural, I mean tasteless, but beyond that to their rest-less technique.

The reader will undoubtedly be able to feel now which way the anti-musicological, anti-problematic wind is blowing. There is no question that the possibility (though not necessarily the actuality) of reducing audible slides was opened up by Spohr's chin-rest; before that, glissando must have been a necessary, constant part of violin technique, accompanying all but the very closest changes of position. It follows that if there was any difference in this respect between pre-classical (and classical) times and the romantic and post-romantic era after Spohr, it must have been the latter that used less glissando – while for Bach, continual, 'romantic' sliding would have been an absolute must; he would have been as little able to conceive of slideless changes of position as of the grand piano, which the musicologists do not view with equal favour. It further follows that as a genius who had acquired a supremely articulate mode of expression, he must have made creative allowance for, must have incorporated slides in the very process of composition, must have used them as an expressive means, heeding the need for them even more than the need for the singer's breathing – for breathe you often can in many places, whereas slide you often can only in one. And indeed, once we reinspect his prominent fiddle parts, especially (though not exclusively) the slow movements of the two solo concertos and the (D minor) double concerto, we easily find how he composed structurally logical slides into the music. And then we recall Bronislaw Huberman's great performances of the solo concertos (which are extant on gramophone records) and realize that even the inspired slides in the outer movements of the A minor may have been part of Bach's own intention, and that even if they weren't, Bach would have been delighted to hear them.

Another problem of authenticity which musicology has created without remotely solving it is that of actual tone production. It is downright bizarre to observe how strenuous efforts are being made to re-establish the precise sound (though not, perhaps the precise faulty intonation) of the pre-classical era, without some elementary differences between 'them' and 'us' being taken into account. For one thing, there is, tonally, an incisive difference between gut strings and the later varieties, gut with steel around it or altogether gutless. I have, occasionally, heard 'authentic performances' with gut Ds and gut As, but the stunning difference between steel E (the only E-string we know) and gut E is almost invariably left out of account. Yet, compared to that difference, most of the differences that are being heeded result in not much more than pedantic changes.

For another, more important and indeed more complex thing, there is this question of vibrato versus senza vibrato: many are the 'authentic', largely vibrato-less performances all of us have heard which, in the end, bored the pants off even the most maniacal pursuer of authenticity if he had any ears left; you often lose them in the chase, which seems to be considered a small price to pay for entry into the paradise of the past, though some of us might regard it as the supreme sacrifice. The puzzle for those of us who have not elevated boredom to a supreme virtue is – why is it all so painfully monotonous? Is string vibrato really as important as all that? Or are our ears corrupted, as musicological players and listeners never tire of telling us – or rather, they do tire, for they fall asleep as helplessly as does the rest of us. The answer is not easy, but it is simple nevertheless; only wrong answers are complicated.

Even in classical times and indeed for the greater part of the nineteenth century, vibrato was not employed as a matter of course; it was confined to what they used to call 'expressive notes'. Now, I have plentiful experience in coaching classical string quartets on the very highest level – by which I mean, in the present context, that the players in question were fully equipped technically, had the entire repertory of contemporary tone-production at their easy disposal. Though I would never dream of insisting on authentic playing (because I refuse to accept that, in terms of actual sound and its experience, we can possibly tell what authentic playing is), I concede happily that there are places, quite especially in the late Beethoven quartets, where vibrato-less tone seems an absolute requirement; indeed, at the Summer School of Music in Dartington, my friend Rudolf Kolisch and I were diametrically opposed quartet teachers because, for example, he insisted on Beethoven's Razumovsky Quartets being played on the string throughout. It is, in fact, both depressing and paradoxical to have to remind oneself that while we claim that the range of expressive means is getting ever wider in modern times, the range of string tone has actually narrowed: where the player of the past had the entire spectrum from senza vibrato to molto vibrato at his disposal, the contemporary player makes do with a chronic vibrato which changes character but little, and which indeed is often used for negative purposes – to gloss over any inadequacies of intonation.

However, on almost every single occasion when I requested or suggested vibrato-less tone, and even though the suggestion may have been enthusiastically accepted in theory, I came to regret it bitterly: the tone produced turned out to be artificial – the right hand, which used to be tone-producer-in-chief until, roughly, the 1930s, playing an all too passive part in the somewhat embarrassed (and, frankly, embarrassing) operation. In short, I wished I had never spoken, and tried to find a euphemism for 'Forget it!' – which, by players of high quality and deep insight, was gratefully accepted.

The moral is close to being self-explanatory. We can no longer play without vibrato: the art has been lost. Our string teaching does

not, to any extent, include vibrato-less playing, the finer shades of
vibrato-less playing, dependent as they are on a more or less
exclusive concentration on the tone-producing and tone-shading,
tone-modulating capacities of the right hand. Under the influence of
the development of vibrato which, since Fritz Kreisler, has been
potentially all-pervasive, the tone-shaping powers of the right hand
have, inevitably, atrophied to some considerable extent. Kreisler,
totally individualistic in his own, sharply characteristic tone-
production (he only used the upper two-thirds of the bow) was the
first to employ vibrato in quick passages (without any diminution of
clarity), and we've never heard the end of it, although we definitely
have heard the end of the primacy of the right hand, which would be
a condition of meaningful vibrato-less playing. We do, of course, get
musicological education in vibrato-less playing nowadays – which,
however, tends to be a conspiracy of the musically and/or instru-
mentally less talented, the hard-of-hearing leading the hard-of-
hearing, or the limping leading the limping, and it's not only one
hand that limps, it is both. Speaking purely empirically, I therefore
submit that the musicologist's non-vibrato is as much of a delusory
solution of his self-created problems as is the slideless performance,
if for entirely different reasons.

What the two have in common, nevertheless, is the primacy of
musicology over music – which, in this age of musical insecurity, is a
godsend to many an anxious soul. I have repeatedly made the social
experiment of telling one or the other faithful about some of my
greatest musical experiences he cannot possibly have shared, such as
Huberman's afore-mentioned interpretation of Bach's A minor Concerto (but in the flesh), Furtwängler's and Mengelberg's *Matthew
Passions*, or again Furtwängler playing the cadenza, on the piano, of
course, of the D major Brandenburg – all performances on whose
total unmusicologicality the listener to my stories could safely
depend. Without exception, the reaction was one of overriding,
retrospective prejudice: though courtesy may have prevented one or
the other addressee from saying so in so many words, I was advised,
in effect, that it just can't have been any good. However, be it said in
honour of one musicologist, Basil Lam,★ that when I played him a

---

★(Basil Lam, one of the author's colleagues at the BBC, was also a professional
harpsichord player; the Basil Lam Ensemble gave several broadcasts on the BBC's
Third Programme. Ed.)

tape of that Furtwängler cadenza which was floating around at the BBC, he immediately succumbed to the power of the performance and did not even suggest that had Furtwängler but played the cadenza on the harpsichord, it would have been still better: he was aware that it would run the risk of becoming as artificial as contemporary vibrato-less violin-playing tends to be – which is not to say, of course, that there are not, by now, great harpsichordists, the proportion being considerably smaller than that of great fiddlers amongst violinists or great pianists amongst pianists, because the proportion of harpsichordists who have become what they are for the wrong – i.e. not purely musical – reasons is, in inverse ratio, high.

The central part that criticism plays in musicology is not so much evidenced by its preoccupation with textual criticism which, after all, is merely a sifting of the true from the unrecognizedly untrue, as by the primacy of musicology over music if and when it occurs – and in practice, albeit not in theory, it occurs all the time. The musicologist, that is to say, once again stands or falls, in his own eyes as well as in the eyes of the ever-increasing congregation of orthodox believers (ears, we have seen, don't always come into it), with his knowing better than the musician – and his main object of criticism is not, in fact, his material, but the musical evil-doer; or, to put it a little more realistically from the psychological point of view, he turns the musician into his material. There is not, I suggest, a single outstanding musician around who, at least in private, and when there are no musicological microphones under the table, does not bitterly complain about the influence of musicology on our musical culture: when these lines are in print, not one of them will send a letter to the press in straightforward defence of the discipline. On the contrary, they usually put the case more radically than I do; to them, it tends to appear as a simple alternative: it's either you or me, musicology or music, there isn't room for both of us.

4 Other Phoney Professions

(i) The Professional Broadcaster

Our preliminary skirmishes into music are almost over, but our list of phoney professions, while not designed to be complete, has to go well beyond the professions I enumerated at Tenerife* in order to complete my picture of the elemental role which criticism inevitably plays in any phoney profession you care to think of. However, one such profession which I did list on that occasion is still outstanding; in fact, it was the 'professional broadcaster' on whom I concentrated when I addressed those professional broadcasters, and it was they who provided me with what I have so far found to be the most illuminating reactions to my thesis.

I suggested to them that the professional broadcaster has done untold harm to the arts, and could do untold good to them – if professional broadcasters could bring themselves to have the kind of insight which I expected from my genius witch-pricker who never was. I put it to them that as in all the other phoney professions, it was terribly easy to distinguish between a radio man who accepted his profession's phoniness and one who fought its bogus aspects.

The radio man who accepts his profession's phoniness knows that radio is a means, not an end. He may or may not talk in terms of 'good broadcasting' (the phoneys always do), but when he does, he does not mean to say that good broadcasting is a primary aim, to which the art of music, or any other art, has to adjust. He does not, in fact, talk about 'the art of broadcasting' at all: this delusion is reserved for the phonily professional broadcaster who knows in his heart of hearts that if he were not a broadcaster, he would be

*See p. 13.

nothing at all – and how many of them there are! It is he who creates all the problems of broadcasting, ever more insoluble, to which hundreds of highly paid hours are devoted in conference every year; it is he who has forgotten that the broadcasting of a late Beethoven quartet, as distinct from the vibrato-less playing of one of its emotionally contained passages, simply is no problem so long as the broadcast is straightforward, without any gimmicks and without any twaddle, in which case it can be turned into a major artistic event – because in the studio as distinct from the concert hall, you can establish *chamber*-musical acoustic conditions: the players can play to each other as they are intended to, and the listeners can, acoustically, hearingly, become one of them.

I speak with almost twenty years' inside knowledge of the history of broadcasting when I say that it has shown beyond any shadow of doubt that where music has been made to serve broadcasting, instead of broadcasting serving music, the ultimate result has been failure, even though there may have been temporary, journalistic success. Of course, it has happened that the attempt to make music serve broadcasting has failed journalistically because the music in question proved too strong to be turned into a servant – and in such cases, there has been artistic success. But all those compositions which, allegedly, were specially written for broadcasting, intrinsically bound up with it, can be shown to have failed artistically in proportion as they succeeded in their phoney aim – to serve the non-existent art of broadcasting.

Broadcasting is a craft, not an art. There is only one conceivable distinguishing characteristic of an art, and that is a specific system of communication (call it language if you must, though every language I know is translatable, whereas every art I know isn't) through which new truths are conveyed which could not possibly be conveyed, or be conveyed to anything like the same extent, by means of any other system. The phoney broadcasting professional, because he has no truths inside him anyhow, because he is the second-hander *par excellence* and knows it, debases the concept of art in an unsuccessful attempt to elevate the craft of broadcasting.

Of course, it is quite often said that more than one leading composer has written music specifically for radio, welcoming the opportunities which the new art of broadcasting proffered to the creative musician. Yes, that has happened, though the welcome not only sounded hollow, but, in due course, proved hollow. Those leading composers, that is to say, weren't leading anybody or anything when they accepted or undertook such a task; and once they had established themselves in the world of music and gained financial as well as artistic self-respect, they forgot all about the art of broadcasting – every single one of them did. Their specific radio music, meanwhile, has survived, or not, according to the degree of its musical weight alone. The situation is clear, unambiguous: can we name a single well-established composer who has reached middle age, and who has kept alive what seemed his early enthusiasm for radiogenic music? And even if we believe that we can actually think of one, we find that the work in question could just as well be reproduced on disc or tape for home use, and therefore has nothing to do with a distinguishable art of broadcasting at all – nor, of course, with any specific art of the gramophone, or with the art of the loudspeaker.

Again, mixed media – where they exclude the visual dimension – *seem*, of course, eminently suitable for radio broadcasting, but broadcasting must remember that it is really *it* that is eminently suitable for *them* if it doesn't want to go megalomaniac (which, on the higher salary levels, it easily does): it is a channel, a means of communicating something that can be communicated without it. Chamber music seems eminently suitable for a chamber, but that doesn't turn the chamber into an art form.

As the chairman, for well over ten years, of an international working party of the European Broadcasting Union,★ I have been in the – scientifically – privileged position of being able to gain more than superficial insight into the working of countless radio organizations, not only European: for one thing, there are one or two extra-European stations which are Full Members of the Union, while for another, there are the very active Associate Members like the United States and Canada. Now, I give it as my highly informed opinion that there isn't a radio organization in the world where managerial radio planners and music departments don't think of each other as a bit of a rum lot: professional broadcasters

---

★'My' committee – revolting convention of using the personal pronoun! – has been planning the EBU International Concert Seasons ever since their inception in 1968. I consider most chairmanship phoney too, not to speak of 'leadership': I believe in horizontal management and organization and don't think that I know better. We have never had a row or even the slightest friction.

and professional musicians usually, thoughtlessly, unimaginatively, mediocrely spend their sterile time arguing what they think are their conflicting interests. A plague on both their houses, I say: the musician who entrenches himself upon an anti-radio position removes himself, in that respect, as much from reality as does his pet adversary, the professional broadcaster. My tiny example of radio's new chamber home for the string quartet shows how one can achieve a confluence of aims where there was conflict, a total amalgam of a radiogenic and a musico-genic exercise – and the example could be diversely multiplied; in fact, I did multiply it in Tenerife in careful detail.

But the fact remains that it is the professional broadcaster, his phoniness, that is the initiator of the conflict, the creator of a pseudo-problem in whose development, and in the prevention of whose solution, the radio musician then plays an all too willing part – instead of resting content, securely and creatively so, with being a musician who has mastered the minor craft of handling a mass medium. Subjected to the professional broadcaster's constant criticism, more or less outspoken – for this phoney professional, too, depends for his very professional life on knowing better – the radio musician, unless he has strength of character and, equally important, the clarity of will, will soon try to turn himself into a professional broadcaster too, instead of trying amiably to bring the professional broadcasters to their senses; after all, promotion may be involved.

At Tenerife, I did not mention the critical element, the *sine qua non* of the professional broadcaster's existence, which is precariously balanced on his one-upmanship *vis-à-vis* the true professional, be he musician or drama expert or a member of any other so-called 'supply department'. The very term establishes the professional broadcaster's superiority: you supply; I, the customer, the representative of the public, call the tune, however banal the melody may be. My responsibility is greater, wider (read: my salary is higher) than yours; it is my duty to know better.

The course of events after my address showed that there was no need to call the professional broadcaster's professionally critical attitude towards those with inner authority by its name; perhaps it was even fortunate that I did not articulate my view on this steady stream of criticism which, immediately after I had finished, turned into a torrent – but also turned the other way, inward, turned into spontaneous self-criticism by leading professional broadcasters, the very last thing I should have expected.

Of course, they did not beat their breasts, nor did they verbalize their self-criticisms – about which, nevertheless, there was no doubt, as one or two very young German radio people laughingly reminded me. What happened was that when I had concluded my tolerably sober remarks, there was an explosion of sustained applause, which was not the form at all: no previous speaker had been applauded, since the whole thing was supposed to be a conference rather than a public event. I had felt the waves all along, while I spoke, but though they greatly encouraged me, my internal prognosis was that they would remain waves, perhaps with an appreciative murmur (as well as a hostile murmur) here and there, without the conventions of the conference being upset.

That was not all, nor indeed was it the most illuminating part of the meeting's reaction which, if my thesis had got across at all, was bound to be ambivalent. As one of those young, anti-authoritarian, anti-authoritative Germans later put it to me in private, the next stage, at which the applauders had to cope with the trauma, was bound to be (and I quote them): 'For heaven's sake, what have I done? I've applauded an attack on myself! Order has to be re-established. I have to explain (save) myself.' And introverted aggression was duly extroverted again: at the ensuing question time and discussion time, many of the most passionate applauders (I had observed them closely) started criticizing my submission with almost the same fervour with which, wordlessly, they had applauded it. And indeed, the rest of the conference was marked by the trauma: where, previously, not a single speaker had referred to a previous speaker, all the papers having been carefully prepared, there now was not a single speaker who did not refer to my speech and, in particular, to the concept of the phoney professional broadcaster. Most of the references were jocular, to be sure, by the way, by way of incidental entertainment, but the very fact that they occurred as if ordered by (psychological) law, that carefully scripted papers had to be interrupted in order to make room for them, showed that my addressees had received the diagnostic message. Even the final, ultra-official after-luncheon speech did not fail to include a much-appreciated, humorously defensive reference to phoncy professionals.

Though most of my colleagues thought that on the whole, the

conference had been, if not a failure, a waste of time, I could not hide my intellectual elation from myself, though I successfully concealed it from everybody else: for the first time, I thought, phoney professionals had realized, however momentarily, their own phoniness – had realized the vapidity of their sternly critical attitude towards a group of people some of whom actually knew better, had the inner authority. As a confrontation between outer and inner authority, the occasion was an ethical feast. For the rest, to my knowledge, only one acknowledged professional broadcaster reacted to my thesis by taking a practical, indeed professional step in the wrong direction – that of upsetting the stringently defined concept of proper broadcasting organization: the Head of Music of the Israel Broadcasting Authority distributed copies of my speech amongst all music producers.

(ii) The Editor

Proper broadcasting organization: how did it all start? The question leads us straight to the next phoney profession, that of the editor. Sir William Haley was Editor of *The Times* before he became Director-General of the BBC, and the BBC's division into 'Planning' and 'Supply', into professional broadcasters and those who had better be, is his invention entirely: the model was the organization of a newspaper, with the editorial staff on the one hand and the writers, the actual contributors, on the other. Since the BBC was – and, up to a realistically definable point, still is – the model for the rest of the broadcasting world, Haley can justly be hailed as the discoverer of a phoney profession.

I am not sneering – not altogether. The inbuilt friction between Planning and Supply has yielded many a valuable result. The spirit behind it all is vaguely democratic: let them fight it out. The trouble is that in the fight between the government (Planning) and the opposition (Supply), the opposition can never hope to take over.

No matter, I am not here concerned with the best way of organizing broadcasting stations (much as I should like to be, and not only after a double whisky or two), but with what the phoney professions can tell us about the nature of criticism. Amongst them, the editor, a blood relation of the professional broadcaster, assumes a distinguished position: the entire reading world, such as it is, depends on him – with the exception of my humble self, who has stopped reading newspapers, apart from the sports pages.

For the past quarter of a century, I have contributed to 200-odd newspapers, journals, magazines, etc., in two languages – and thus been responsible to 200-odd editors. At the same time, and for the same period of time, I have continually been an editor, in sundry different areas. I don't think editing is anything to write home about; on the contrary, what I am saying is that I have enough experience to state, with that much-revered outer authority (which does not necessarily exclude inner authority), that what much of conventional editing boils down to is interference with the writer.

The editor is at his best, therefore, when he realizes that, unless he is careful, heedless of calcified journalistic law and custom, he is bound to be at his worst – his most unobtrusively destructive, creating problems of 'style' and practical desirability which he proceeds to solve to his own or his boss's satisfaction, and nobody else's: nobody else is in on the act. In fact, the reader, to whom the editor purports to be responsible, is never given a chance to discover what has been solved, or has remained unsolved.

Editorial choice – of contributor or contribution – is, of course, a real activity which the world of printed and spoken communication cannot do without: I am not implying that this part of the editor's function is phoney, or if anything is deceptive about it, it is the description of the activity, 'editing' being a clear, or rather confused, misnomer for an activity which has nothing to do with the original meaning of the word* or its later, specific meaning.† In short, I cannot see why the chooser shouldn't be called Chooser, even where the editor in question turns out to be a beggar so far as his more important contributions are concerned – which he frequently does. The Germans, at least, differentiate between the *Herausgeber* (the literal equivalent of the word 'editor') and the *Redakteur*, who is in charge of all the phoney aspects of editing, which pass under the euphemisms of 'revision', 'correction', 'clarification' and so forth, but, more often than not, amount to wilful changes to which the writer may or may not have given his agreement – not to speak of cuts which, if the original piece is any good at all, are bound to result in distortions or suppressions of

*To publish.
†To select, choose.

meaning. Although the mediocre editor is not aware of the fact, it is for this very reason that he prefers a mediocre piece to a good piece: it's easier to cut.

On tape, cutting and inter-cutting by the editing producer can, of course, result in a total reshaping of the original contribution, if not indeed in a rethinking of it: the contributor, the speaker, is degraded, reduced to the role of a provider of material for the editing producer to get his 'art of broadcasting' to work on it. In a newspaper, such ultimate mutilation is not so easy, except where the 'material' is an interview or a reported speech. Innumerable are the instances, nevertheless, of important individual contributions being standardized according to the 'style' of a newspaper – and this so-called style includes such aspects as titles and subtitles (more often than not the editor's rather than the writer's, who sees 'his' title for the first time when the paper is out), paragraphing (as if this were not a function of structure, the author's own structure), punctuation (which likewise should be a function of structure, part of the author's meaning therefore), polysyllabicophobia (this one I invented specially for the more primitive newspaper reviews of my book – a gift), spelling (e.g. -ize v. -ise) and, perhaps most important, tone: each editor creates his own problems about what would give offence to whom and 'solves' it by cutting or changing the allegedly offending passage, the whole operation usually being expressive of nothing but his or his boss's personality, unless more primitive motives (such as fear of advertisers and/or of loss of circulation) are involved; in any case, the protected party is never asked his opinion: the editor decides what's good for him.

Throughout my editing life, which has covered both the printed and the publicly spoken word, I have refused to play the phoney game. Revisions, improvements, clarifications are suggested to the author, with reasons when necessary; if he doesn't like them, he is not pressed to accept them. The necessity for cuts, where it arises, is simply pointed out; if he wants to try his own hand at them, he is welcome. If he wants me to take over, I do – but not without submitting every single cut to his considered approval.

The same principle underlies my approach to the editing side of the production of a recorded concert or recital – and the public does not realize what falsehoods are committed by responsible, or formerly responsible musicians who are trying to turn themselves into professional broadcasters and become equally professional editors on the way. I have heard broadcasts of tapes in which expositions of sonata movements had been copied in order to replace a repeat which seemed faulty to the producer – as if there were any artistic point to a repeat if it was not a subtle variation on the first-time exposition, alive, throughout, to the fact that the first-time exposition has happened and is a thing of the past. I have heard broadcasts of recorded public concerts in which the repeat of such an exposition was simply deleted in order to ‘fit the show neatly into a predetermined space and thus please, not the art of music or its performing servants, but the professional broadcasters who put planning efficiency above all else, since they don’t understand anything else anyway. Far from being prepared to do any such thing, I will, if I notice in the editing channel that, say, a general pause is musically too long, ring the performers and whistle this excerpt to them, suggesting an infinitesimal cut, again illustrated by whistling. Without their immediate approval, I shall never dream of exercising what would be editorial irresponsibility.

The reason for this autobiographical report is not to show what a wonderful editor I am. On the contrary, what I am demonstrating is that however lousy I may be, from the ‘professional’ standpoint from which these editorial practices are invariably defended, I got away with it with the greatest ease – and what is more positively rewarding is that highly substantial contributors respond to my invitations where they don’t want to work for more ‘professional’ editors.

As for newspapers, journals, and magazines, I wish to be taken seriously when I ask this rhetorical question: who wants them to have a unified ‘style’ anyway, at the expense of their contributors’ individualities? Who buys the *Guardian* because it spells ‘realise’, or *The Times* because it spells ‘realize’? Who cares? One or two people do: they think that ‘-ise’ is a much-needed standardization, or, alternatively, they think that the precisest possible, widest possible differentiation is one of the functions of any developed language, whence the difference between ‘-ise’ and ‘-ize’ ought to be retained – and not abolished the other way round either, as is American wont (‘analyze’). But those who care one way or the other, or who care about the problem without – can you blame them? – having come to a definite conclusion, would like to see writers’ practices, not editorial practices: they’d be interested to learn which contributors to the *Guardian and The Times* write ‘-ise’, and which ‘-ize’ – and that goes, more weightily, for less trivial differences in personal writing style. Real problems would thus be exposed, and the editor's phoney problems abolished – problems whose 'solutions' are introduced at the expense of writer and reader alike. Are you interested in the title a sub-editor gives to your favourite reviewer's piece? Are you interested in his re-paragraphing, his cuts, his occasional tactful change of words? Wouldn't you, at least, prefer him to be called Changer rather than Editor? The honest job description would raise the problem of the editor's problems in bright daylight – and why shouldn't you raise it? You are the customer. So am I, which is why I have virtually stopped reading newspapers.

When, in the middle of my Preface, we arrived at Gatwick Airport, I bought myself a *Guardian* – because it contained a document which I was going to use in this section, i.e. my review of Saul Bellow's book, *To Jerusalem and Back*. About a week before, the Literary Editor of the *Guardian* had rung me and asked me whether, in spite of my impending departure, I could review the book: he thought it might stimulate something – which, in due course, it did, but not quite the way he wanted it to stimulate me.

As a contributor, I like the *Guardian* and its Literary Editor: phoniness there is minimal (which, with respect, is still a lot). As in the *Spectator* (but not, say, in the *Sunday Times*), you invent your own titles. Your paragraphs are respected, as indeed is your individuality; and if you adhere to the 'wordage' you are being given, there will be no cuts. If any changes are thought desirable, you will, invariably, be respectfully consulted in the first place.

The telephone call came at the most inopportune moment imaginable. I had rigidly planned my time-table before our departure, including as it had to a more than normal (ten hour) load of BBC work, a lecture at the University of Leicester which necessitated my staying there overnight, a football article for the *Spectator*, an obituary on Deryck Cooke, a large-scale piece on Willi Schuh's new book on Richard Strauss's early years for the *Frankfurter Allgemeine Zeitung* (who do invent your titles), and indeed Part III, Section 2, which had to reach its publisher or, rather, pre-publisher, before I left. I never accept the excuse (my own, that is) of having 'no time' for something that ought to be done, but on this occasion, I really thought that for once, the excuse might be justifiable. Or might it? I was going to a football match on Saturday, and to a dinner party on Sunday. If I cancelled both, the job could be done.

The Literary Editor thanked me profusely and brought the book along to my office on the day of his call. Now, it must be realized that I am not a proper professional book reviewer at all, however many the books I am presumptuous enough to review. The professional book reviewer reads an enormous number of books, except for those he is reviewing. I don't read any books (I've read them), except for those I am reviewing. The trouble was, then, that I actually read *To Jerusalem and Back*, every word of it. When my review reached the Literary Editor, he rang me again and thanked me, not quite so profusely. There was anxiety in his voice – all the more so since he knew about my rush. Here is the review as it appeared:★

IT IS A long time since a Knut Hamsun received the Nobel Prize for literature. Or perhaps one should say, more cautiously and hence with a greater degree of certitude, that it is a long time since a Nobel prize winner wrote as bad a book as this one – as sub-journalistic, shallow, mistake-ridden and, yes, intellectually irresponsible.

I started reading it with a great deal of potential identification. Both Bellow and I are Jews and, without concrete link with the faith, enthusiastically Jewish. For both of us, Israel is an elemental experience – the answer to extermination. And the City of Jerusalem invited both of us, with our wives, to stay at the Mishkenot Sha'ananim, the dwellings of serenity, to think and write in inspiring surroundings, as peaceful as they are warful.

He has been; we're going next year. He wrote this book there – which hit me just at the right moment: it is being accorded a place of honour in an intellectual life rich in anti-models. I know now what and how not to write in Jerusalem, and there is nothing as productive as a clear knowledge of what not to do – a fact of which the experienced author of the Ten Commandments was well aware during his own Sinai campaign: he centred them on ten negative warnings.

Bellow calls his 'a personal account', God knows why. It is, largely, an impersonal account of what other people have thought and think about Israel and the problem of the Middle East, from Sartre through Kissinger, and sundry Israelis to Bellow's university pal Morris Janowitz in Chicago. As for his own views, Bellow proudly presents them as those of an amateur, which is why, on the whole, he modestly confines himself to trivia and wrong facts.

By page 10, we know all about the 'delicate light' and the 'thought-nourishing air' of Jerusalem, but on p. 93, having run out of thought despite all the nourishment, he's off again as if nothing had happened:

★(See Appendix Note 1. Ed.)

'the air of Jerusalem feeds the intellect – one of the great rabbis believed this', nor does he 'forbid himself the reflection' that Jerusalem's light 'may be the outer garment of God', in which case the London fog is probably the underpants. Even if you are able to project profundity on to such kitsch, one round of it should be enough.

Didn't the publisher notice? As a matter of fact, he has noticed nothing – not even the fact that the Mendelssohn Violin Concerto is in E minor and not in E major. Apropos of a master class held by Isaac Stern and Alexander Schneider, that is to say, we are first regaled with an explanation of the Russian-Jewish fiddling phenomenon ('a death-defying act on four taut strings by means of which you save your life'), and then with the position of the Mendelssohn Concerto in Bellow's inner life: 'For a long time now, I've disliked it. I'm down on all this silvery whickering.' A colour-blind person on painting would be no emptier than the key-deaf, or rather mode-deaf, Bellow is on music. Among men of his stature, he must be alone in not knowing the Eleventh Commandment, negative again: Thou Shalt Know when to Shut Up.

For the rest, my mind is made up. The book I shall write at the Mishkenot Sha'ananim will be on the Mendelssohn Violin Concerto, arguably the greatest of them all.

Even when it comes to sheer reporting on leading Israeli figures, some of the most essential facts are simply omitted. There is a lot of prattle about the High Court Judge Chaim Cohn and his (unnamed) wife Michal, but we are not told that this towering man is so unconditional an opponent of capital punishment that he had to disqualify himself from the Eichmann trial which he had been appointed to conduct and that Michal Smoira-Cohn is the Israel Broadcasting Authority's Head of Music (and, incidentally, the former wife of Eli Goren, one of the BBC Symphony Orchestra's leaders). This, on the most elementary level, is bad journalism.

But when too much is said and nothing is done, the fact remains that the book will make people think about the problem of Israel, even if it is not Bellow's own thoughts that will make them think.

It wasn't quite the review expected of a book by a writer who had won the Nobel Prize for literature the other week. Be it said in the Literary Editor's favour that he had read the book himself, and that he readily agreed that it wasn't exactly a masterpiece. But three things worried him. First, in paragraph four, last line, could he perhaps 'just change three letters' and turn 'trash' into 'trivia'? They had, after all, planned the review as a tribute to the Nobel Prize winner. The sun broke through and I agreed. I agreed, that is, that the change would not, fundamentally, affect my meaning; more potently, I agreed that I needn't be all *that* harsh on Saul Bellow or indeed the *Guardian*: I frankly pitied both of them – aside from the fact that I was, at that moment, preoccupied with slightly more burning problems. The fact remains that 'trash' was what I meant and, more important, that trash is what, I submit, Bellow produced in this instance; the 'kitsch' demonstrated in paragraph five was designed to link up with the concept.

Secondly, the Literary Editor suggested, a sentence I had written about Elias Canetti was very hard indeed on Saul Bellow: he, the Literary Editor himself, only knew *Auto-da-fé* and *Crowds and Power*, and he couldn't even find Canetti, a resident in this country until a short while ago, in *Who's Who*. That, I did not say, was not my problem, but a typically phoney editorial problem: the whole German-speaking world (I did say) was aware of Canetti the playwright as well as of his other, extremely diverse writings. I know the man well enough to be able to say that he would never describe himself as a novelist or a psychologist in the first place: how could he, with one book each? Anyhow, with the sun still shining, I agreed to drop this particular sentence.

Lastly, the Literary Editor said, quite overcome by my unprecedented willingness to accommodate, this could at least be said in the book's favour – that it would make people think, or think again, about Israel's problems. 'True,' I said, 'but it won't be Bellow who'll make them think; it'll be what he quotes and cites. However, if you like, I'll dictate you a last sentence and paragraph to that effect. I mean, I won't "dictate", I'll shyly suggest.' 'Shyly suggest!' he said bitterly, or teasingly, or a bit of both. 'What, *now*?' he asked, as I was about to commence. 'Of course. What's done is done; here goes.' And I dictated the last paragraph.

By now, the Literary Editor was so delighted at my accepting not only one suggestion, but all three of them (I had heard in his voice that the most he had hoped for were the first two) that he hardly noticed that this last paragraph, far from being a compliment, rubbed in the utter unoriginality of the book.

Advisedly, I have chosen this civilized example of editorial intervention – where other writers, for other papers, have to suffer brutal interference – in order to show the, I hope, less than gentle reader that even on this level of apparent reasonableness, the editor creates problems he fails to solve. His victims are, first, the necessary object of his criticism, the writer than whom he has to know better, and, second, the reader. Judge for yourself: what have you, the customer, gained or lost? Have the problems been solved for you? Maybe I am to blame too; maybe if I hadn't been under such pressure of work, I should have accumulated the necessary aggressive energy to prevent the sun from breaking through at the wrong moment. The replacement of 'trash' by 'trivia' may be trivial, but the deletion of the passage about Canetti did withhold utterly factual information from you, which, if you were interested in that writer at all (who, of late, has won sundry prizes and honours in German-speaking countries),★ you would have been grateful for. As for that last sentence, it did not even solve the editor's own problem, and if the intention was to make the book a slightly more acceptable proposition, it can safely be said that you did not buy the book because of it. What you did buy if you bought the paper was a review by a writer in whom you are interested (otherwise you wouldn't have bought or borrowed this book and read it up to the present stage), without getting precisely what he had intended to tell you.

Conversely, what has anybody gained? The editor, a little peace of mind, for the wrong reasons – for Saul Bellow, I am sure, couldn't have cared less about such amendments in the context of a devastating review; he might even have appreciated the information about Canetti, whose only novel he admires, and of whom he only knows two books. So far as the editing part of his job is concerned, then, the editor moves in dreamland, more often than not – fancying himself as the realist at the same time, who has to bring the contributor down to earth when necessary.

(iii) The Politician

The only reason why the politician might not be able to qualify as a phoney in our sense is that especially with the younger generations, he has lost esteem to such an extent that political life, however honestly attempted, is becoming very difficult for all interested parties. Nor need one dive into the sub-culture, the anti-culture, the alternative culture – or whichever fancy name you choose for

---

★(In 1981, Canetti was awarded the Nobel Prize for literature. Ed.)

the anti-establishment establishment, as if one establishment weren't enough – in order to discover widespread contempt for the politician; it isn't only the anarchists that have found out that there is something wrong with all established and envisaged -archies and -cracies. If you are acquainted with contemporary university life, you are aware that very few of the most intelligent young people have any intention of going into politics nowadays (nor, by the way, into broadcasting!), and when you speak at the Oxford Union or Cambridge Union, you are plunged into a smiling game about the past as never before – an exercise in that self-irony which seems to have lost not only ideals, but the very need for ideals.

Nevertheless, it is politicians who rule us, and so long as we appoint them and pay them, we shall have to face the charge of respecting them; if we sneer at them at the same time, we merely evince an unresolved ambivalence towards parent figures which has this to be said against it – that as distinct from our real parents, the politicians owe their place to us, without our proving capable of putting them in their place – an attempt reserved, it seems, for the present section.

The cataclysmic dishonesty, that is to say, that is part and parcel of the professional equipment of a politician is never honestly faced – just because we don't know whom or what to put in his place: the human mind finds it difficult to acknowledge the existence of unsolvable problems; if and when they are encountered, they are denied. So necessary a part is lying and deceit of the very fabric of politics as we know it, autocratic or democratic, that with the possible exception of the witch-pricker and the critic, the politician is perhaps the only figure who is not only a phoney professional, but indeed a professional phoney – who, yet again, depends for his professional life on knowing better, though he is wellnigh alone even amongst phoney professionals in almost invariably knowing worse, which is why he needs advisers and the sub-structure of some civil service or other: once they have dealt with any practical problem in hand, one asks oneself what he is there for, except to mess it all up again.

Mind you, he is there for Parliament, or is supposed to be; in reality, Parliament is there for him, not for us, whoever 'we' are: one of the fundamental flaws of democracy, which again we don't own up to because dictatorship and autocracy and totalitarianism are immeasurably worse, is that the majority is usually, though not invariably, wrong, and that throughout the history of mankind, both ethical and cognitive achievement has been minority achievement in the first place, invariably opposed by majorities whenever they had the chance, with all the moral and moralizing power which a majority, which is mistaken for reality, inevitably commands.

In Parliament, political life is supposed to be at its most mature, responsible, effective, realistic. But is it? The very term 'Parliamentary debate' is an intolerable euphemism for a national game wholly removed from reality, and elevated to the emotional status of a ritual: how can a debate be a debate if nobody can change anybody's mind? If nobody on the other side can get up and say, 'Yes indeed, I see what you mean: I was wrong and so was my party. Now how, from your point of view, would you solve problem x? For all I know, we might learn something from you, or at least I might'? Where the rules of the game – the overriding truth of party opinion – are a lie (which, without psychotic denial, ought to be detectable by the most modest intelligence), no truth can easily emerge within it. In Parliament, the power of individual judgement is reduced to a level lower than which only the dictatorships – Fascist or Communist, it doesn't matter – have sunk, because the democratic wrongs of majorities are guaranteed their rightful place on two levels – within parties as well as between them. For the present writer, who has no political allegiances whatever, it was no more than history acting out its more platitudinous truths when a man of extraordinary insight and decency and a staunch believer in individualism to boot, Edward Heath, abysmally failed as a politician – and flowered after he had successfully failed.

It is with the help of Parliament that the politician creates the most effective problems; it is with the help of Parliament that he fails to solve them. That the autocrat does even worse without Parliament says little in its favour, just as a brain tumour says little in favour of a common headache. There is an untold number of such problems; at this sophisticated stage in the devolution of our civilization, it would be an insult to the intelligent reader of this book – it is unlikely that there will be any other – to compose a cumbersome list, since he will be only too ready to supply pertinent examples from his own experience.

One prototypical example, a problem which is likely to burn or, at least, simmer for a long time, must not remain unmentioned, since it is one which not even enlightened minds are quick to identify as the work of politicians, all their own work. It is the problem of inflation. For a long time, I secretly suspected that it was a created problem – too many analagous problems are, which I am professionally more competent to pronounce upon: I am more competent, that is, to pronounce that they were created by one of my own professions, and they will be found all over this section. But during the afore-mentioned lecture tour in Canada in the autumn of 1976, when I rehabilitated American (Buffalo) television towards myself by get-ting up in the middle of the night and watching the most uncom-promising cultural programmes at a sufficiently unearthly time for advertisers not to be interested in interrupting or indeed determining them, I did hear a supreme expert on economics examine the problem of inflation *in extenso* – Milton Friedman, who won the Nobel Prize on the same occasion as did Saul Bellow. Mr Friedman explained that the worldwide problem of inflation was a pseudo-problem, that it would not be difficult at all to eliminate it by (a) cuts in public spending where the government in question did not have the money to spend, and (b) a refusal to print money. He demon-strated how the State of New York, which had allowed itself unsupportable public expenditure, had saved itself when on the brink of disintegration – by being unable to print money. Inflation was always, and necessarily government-induced – a criminal act which amounted to taxation the population hadn't bargained for, and to pushing helpless lower income groups into higher taxation brackets on top of it all. The reduction of unemployment which was its ostensible aim was a deception or an illusion: in the short run, such reduction was indeed achieved and served short-term political ends, but in the long run, unemployment could always be shown to be worse than when the curative measures were introduced. There were no rational grounds at all for reducing inflation: it could simply be abolished, and any government that didn't abolish it – the British government above all – acted immorally.

By spending money he hasn't got, the politician proves himself not only a professional phoney, but a professional charlatan, and I would indeed nominate inflation as the phoney professional's self-created, unsolved problem κατ εξοχην,* were it not for the sinister fact that political inanity, discretion and confidentiality produced in our century what was, arguably, the worst man-made tragedy in the

---

*'Pre-eminently'.

history of the world – the Hitler regime and its consequences. It isn't only that the entire tragedy could easily have been avoided if western politicians had evinced residual intelligence when Hitler occupied the Rhineland, and had promptly intervened, militarily if necessary. That was merely a problem created by stupidity, but worse was to come.

I have long argued that on the analogy of the white lie, the ethical concepts of 'white confidentiality' and 'white discretion' ought to be introduced: confidentiality and discretion, automatically regarded as virtues ('a man of discretion'), are provable vices unless they can be shown to serve an ethical purpose. With quasi-parental, paternalizing secrecy, the children – those not in power – are being kept uninformed about matters, often dangers, that directly concern them – allegedly for their own protection, but in reality for the sole purpose of protecting those in power, be they politicians, leaders of organizations, managements, heads of departments ... Having decided on their course of inaction against the German National Socialists, successive British politicians in power kept their knowledge about what was happening in Germany an absolute secret – for security reasons, for the protection of the state, no doubt, except that nothing could have left the children more insecure, less protected. Fortunately in this major misfortune, there was one child who saw through the parents' act, one politician who suspected the politicians, one witch-pricker who came pretty close to my imaginary witch-pricker of genius – Winston Churchill. Only, in this case, it wasn't a matter of discovering that there weren't any witches; what had to be discovered was that there were. I remember reading, as an early teenager, his insistent analyses of the German situation with admiration – in the *Prager Tagblatt*, Prague's German newspaper which was read all over Europe, and of which my father's brother was the editor.

Once there is a genius witch-pricker, or at least a very talented one, he will not remain without support: anti-phoniness is as attractive as phoniness, if to different people. Senior government servants, weighed down by conflicts within their own minds, eventually decided to commit the unpardonable sin in order to save their souls – 'to pass to Winston Churchill information and secret documents ... about the rising strength and menace of Nazi Germany'.* The next best thing to the elimination of the self-created

---

The Times, 30 November 1976.

problem had started – the concrete education of the man who, single-mindedly if not single-handed, was to save western civilization (whatever his flaws of which we nowadays hear so much, increasingly difficult as we find it to tolerate greatness). 'Mr Ralph Wigram, head of the Foreign Office's central department, had . . . been passing to Churchill dozens of secret documents relating to Germany's military strength, including telegrams from the Ambassador in Berlin, Sir Eric Phipps; detailed analyses of Nazi intentions; and even a dozen secret air ministry memos showing how far Britain's air strength was falling behind Germany's.' You see what I mean by the need for white confidentiality.

That chronic, all-pervasive, all-overriding criticism is an indispensable part of the politician's professional make-up need hardly be demonstrated at length. In a democracy, it is, primarily, criticism of the other party (or parties), whatever it does or thinks; the fact that it's *it* who so acts or thinks proves it wrong. In a totalitarian political system, the object of criticism is without, whereas the underlying illogical principle remains the same; the intelligentsia that is part of the political group in question accepts it without the slightest intellectual difficulty, noticing nothing amiss. Ever since Freud's *Group Psychology and the Analysis of the Ego*,* it has been a sociological commonplace to say that group cohesion depends on a leader and/or a common enemy, but a politician is nothing without a leader (himself, preferably) *and* a common enemy. This means that he is prepared to sacrifice the truth twice over if necessary – to the primacy of leadership and/or the leading ideal, and to the struggle against – the critical degradation of – the common enemy.

(iv) The Psychoanalyst and Psychiatrist

Thomas Szasz has shown that at this point in the history of both capitalist and Marxist society, the psychiatrist and the psycho-

---

*London, 1922. The title is a mistranslation ('mass psychology' would be the equivalent of *Massenpsychologie*) as so many translations of Freudian terms tragically are – including *The Interpretation of Dreams*: 'Dream-reading' would be the closest English replacement for *Traumdeutung*; an interpreter is a translator, but a *Deuter* isn't. A whole concept of psychoanalytic 'interpretation' has developed in the English-speaking world which was never dreamt of in Freud's philosophy. No psychoanalyst has noticed.

analyst easily become the politician's bedfellows, shaping together with him what Szasz calls the 'Therapeutic State' – which, of course, has been more embracingly developed in the United States★ than in Britain, where the phoney concept of mental health does not (yet) play a basic political role: we're always behind the times, thank God. I do not propose to chew the Szaszian cud – the less so since in my last book,† I have closely defined the degree to which I agree with his genuinely revolutionary theses, as well as the respect in which, I think, he has left incomplete his analysis of the psychoanalyst and the psychiatrist. Briefly, I wholly accept his comprehensively argued, central thesis to the effect that the idea of 'mental illness' is, scientifically speaking, no more than a metaphor which has had its day, and which is now used – in America and Soviet Russia alike – for political ends, in order to deprive people of their dignity, if not indeed (in the case of compulsory hospitaliz-ation) their freedom. I have argued‡ that, at the same time, Szasz's most serious omission is his neglect of the psychoanalyst's own psychology: Szasz fights shy of psychologizing intellectual adver-saries, opponents in debate – which is an admirable and indeed scientifically necessary attitude where they cannot logically be proved to be wrong; but a psychological enquiry into what makes your opponent think that twice two makes four and a half is ethically legitimate and logically desirable. In view of the fact that Szasz greeted my entire chapter with enthusiasm, I am assuming that he agreed with my constructive criticism. What I submitted was that the psychoanalyst, inasmuch as he became the victim of what I described as the 'creeping moralism of psychoanalysis', was the agent of his own endo-psychic difficulties.

To the extent that he covertly moralizes, then, and feels the absolute need to evaluate the world as well as his actual patients in terms of what he, or his substitute religion, happens to regard as mentally healthy, his becomes a phoney profession too, creating illusory problems for both individuals (whether his patients or not) and the society that is his imagined patient – without, of course,

---

★Cf. Szasz's *Law, Liberty, and Psychiatry*, London, 1974, pp. 212ff.
†op. cit., 'Psycho-Analytic Congress, 1975' pp. 126ff.
   (*1975* was the author's last book before writing the present one. Meanwhile, *Stravinsky Seen and Heard* (London, Toccata Press, 1982) and *The Great Haydn Quartets* (London, Dent, 1986) have been published. Ed.)
‡ibid.

any possibility of solving them; his brother-in-psychological-arms, the psychiatrist (at times also his internecine enemy) falls into the same category when he, in his turn, replaces the problems he is invited to solve by problems he imposes upon his patients, or other individuals (say, as expert witness in a court of law), or the world at large – problems which, inevitably, hide his own moralizations.

A simple, if well-hidden example of psychoanalytic and psychiatric moralization, to which I have drawn attention in the afore-mentioned place, is the psychoanalytic and psychiatric dogma, or First Commandment, if you like, Thou Shalt Relate – to other people, that is. If you relate, you're normal, or have a chance to be, anyhow; if you don't, you aren't. The 'mental health' of many ex-patients is easily diagnosable by their frantic efforts to relate, often at the expense of doing something reasonable instead for which they would, perhaps, be more gifted. What is worse, the problem of relating now tends to be imposed on the scarcely-born individual from the moment go: post-natal eugenics are practised or recommended which will make the child grow into a 'healthy', relating man. If he marries he's more normal than if he doesn't; if he's got friends he's more normal than if he hasn't; if he decides to propagate the race against what, at the time of writing, are unprecedentedly heavy odds, so that he can relate to his children on top of it all, he's more normal than if he doesn't. I enjoy betting against heavy odds too, but I do try to refrain from regarding those who don't as mentally ill.

A short survey of the history of extreme talent, not to speak of genius, yields a gravely high proportion of non-relaters and limited relaters. To the mediocre psychoanalyst, this is their problem; to me, it is his: if we apply his much-revered reality test to him as well as them, they will pass with flying colours where he will just scrape through, intent upon inventing difficulties for them in order to get rid of his own. 'He must have had difficulties in relating'; that he may have had no difficulties at all in not relating doesn't occur to them. Mozart, if we deduct all sentimental biography which, nowadays, appears in a seductively colourless musicological garb, was the non-relater *par excellence*: the only signs of deep friendship we are allowed to see occur when he needs money.

The world is the typical psychoanalyst's material, then, his object of criticism, and his criticism either degrades by saddling people with his problems (as if they didn't have enough problems of their own), or else 'praises' them without upgrading them – for being able to cope with their problems, their abnormality, which is lovingly defined in the very process of appreciation, and which, in our insecure, fragmented culture, becomes the equivalent of original sin, except that original sin has been found to be more enjoyable. At the same time, it may be argued that when God saddled us with it, that again was His problem, not ours.

The one respect in which our culture resists fragmentation is, in fact, that of psychological values: a science, or pre-science, has been turned inside out, its solemnly anti-moralistic attitude (inconsistently so, to be sure, from the outset) turned into a firm basis for moralizations, and especially for moralizing criticisms, which a vast proportion of people who think that they think for themselves are unknowingly and unthinkingly assimilating even as I write. Psychologizing moralization, like its immediate predecessor, religious moralization, has this inestimable advantage over most other brands of attempted humiliation (if only in your own eyes) of other people – that you can be perfectly, if wrongly sure that you know better: you are at peace with your rotten self, and what more does man, especially psychoanalytic man, desire? As in the case of religion, moreover, moralizations apart, one is in the position of the ultimate truth-finder, so much so that one has an immediate, satisfactory answer, if not to everything – one is too humble or scientifically modest for that – then to every objection, every counter-criticism, every mere attempt at debate. One has thought of them all before; or, if one hasn't, one has mastered the technique of transmuting them into something one has thought of before – or preferably, that St Sigmund has.

Like most saints, he is not above suspicion either, and while I agree with a close psychoanalyst friend of mine that the frenetic contemporary attempts, by so-called detached admirers of Freud's discoveries, to find the warts in his (very honest, if not very human) face are tiresome to say the least, his own role as a phoney professional, as a creator of insoluble problems and moralizing critic of innocent people must not be underestimated – nor must his phoney allegiance to his phoney profession where there was a chance to manifest it – a paradoxical chance, since he himself was persecuted by the phoneys all his life. However, once you have decided to be, and remain a member of a phoney profession, you cannot possibly remain alone, however independent and indeed detested your thought: you need the phoney profession's respectability – and at least some of its objects of destructive criticism. Total intellectual loneliness – the condition for the greatest, the truest, the most helpful the human mind can achieve (discover or invent) – is granted to but few of even the supreme geniuses; Beethoven and Schoenberg were two of them.

Since I last wrote about Szasz in *1975*, he has published a scurrilous book called *Karl Kraus and the Soul-Doctors*.* While it is justly subtitled *A Pioneer Critic and His Criticism of Psychiatry and Psychoanalysis*, it represents a downright grotesque overestimation of Kraus' talent and a grave underplaying of Freud's genius, with which verdict Szasz seems to agree three-quarter-heartedly, pleading a good cause† – which indeed he is pursuing. From our own point of view, incidentally, *A Pioneer Critic of Criticism* would be just as relevant a subtitle: it was the unconfessedly critical attitude of psychoanalysis which Kraus, a coeval of Schoenberg's, seems to have been the first to fight. What, in any case, lifts Szasz's book far above its evaluative distortions is, first, its continued, eloquent crusade for the dignity of man and against its debasers, and secondly, its fearless de-sanctification of Freud – which, purely factual, goes below the warts right down to much-neglected evidence of (as I would say) the phoney professional's inevitable inhumanity, a function, I suggest, of his professional loyalty and indeed discretion: perhaps 'white loyalty' is yet another concept that needs introducing, in that it not only depends on what one is loyal to, but also on whether one is loyal to professional, collective standards which make one sacrifice, again ineluctably, one's concern (if any!) for and about individuals.

So far as his fanatical fight for human dignity is concerned, although Szasz wrongly regards Kraus as an artist, he rightly argues the unconditional dignity of art:‡

> More than any other person, the true artist is, of course, the supporter, interpreter, and mediator of dignity. This is why a great work of art can no more be undignified than a triangle can have four sides. A great work of science or technology can be undignified. Kraus was one of the first among moderns to recognize this fateful fact, and the dangers that lurk behind it.

---

*London, Routledge & Kegan Paul, 1977.
†Private communication.
‡op. cit., p. 161.

As regards the de-canonization of Freud with its proportionate re-dignifying of man, Szasz recalls the psychoanalytic founding father's loyal protection of the world-famed Viennese psychiatrist Julius Wagner-Jauregg – at the expense of a then fashionable object of psychiatric criticism, the so-called 'war neurotics' (in the First World War):

The difference between Kraus's and Freud's attitudes toward Wagner-Jauregg who – as Professor of Psychiatry at the University of Vienna from 1893 to 1928 – was the most prestigious psychiatrist in Austria [right across the metamorphosis of the Austro-Hungarian empire into the little republic of Austria, that is], is displayed dramatically by Freud's defense of Wagner-Jauregg's use of painful electric shocks, euphemistically called 'electrical treatment', on soldiers during the First World War. When the war was over, [Ernest] Jones [the author of the classical Freud biography] related, 'there were many bitter complaints about the harsh, or even cruel, way in which Austrian military doctors had treated the war neurotics, notably in the Psychiatric Division of the Vienna General Hospital of which Professor Julius Wagner-Jauregg was the Director.' [The reference here is to Jones's *The Life and Work of Freud*, vol. III, p. 21.] These complaints led, in 1920, to the appointment by the Austrian War Ministry of a special commission to investigate the charges. [The new liberal era had started, the republic having been proclaimed in 1919.] The commission requested Freud [this was twenty years after *The Interpretation of Dreams* had been published] to submit a memorandum of his expert opinion on this matter. In his memorandum, and also in his personal appearance before the commission, Freud defended Wagner-Jauregg's use of this method of medical torture. The passage in this document most relevant to our present concerns [and to ours!] reads: 'This painful form of treatment introduced in the German army for therapeutic purposes could no doubt also be employed in a more moderate fashion. If it was used in the Vienna Clinics, I am personally convinced that it was never intensified to a cruel pitch by the initiative of Professor Wagner-Jauregg. I cannot vouch for other physicians whom I did not know.' [Szasz's references here are to Freud's *Memorandum on the Electrical Treatment of War Neurotics* (1920) in *The Standard Edition of the Complete Psychological Works of Sigmund Freud*, London, 1953–74, vol. XVII, pp. 213ff., and to Kraus's own satire of the 'electrical treatment' of 'war neurotics' in a fragment on malingerers which Szasz reprints on pp. 150ff. of his book on Kraus.]

Medical criminals, especially of a psychiatric sort, are of course not a special product of the National Socialists or Communists. Interest-

ingly, in his autobiography, Wagner-Jauregg admits to doing what
Freud denied him capable of doing: 'If all the malingerers I cured at
the Clinic, often by harsh enough measures, had appeared as my
accusers, it would have made an impressive trial.' [Quoted in Jones's
biography of Freud, vol. III, p. 23.] Comments Jones: 'Fortunately
for him, as he remarked, most of them were scattered over the former
Austro-Hungarian Empire and were not available, so the Commission ultimately decided in his favor.' [ibid.]

Three shattering facts, rather than mere observations, arise
within the context of our deliberations. First, the esteem which the
phoney professions of psychoanalysis and psychiatry enjoy is high
enough, the saintliness of Freud sufficiently spotless, for this truly
damaging information to have been – not *suppressed* all this time,
for it was freely available, but *re*pressed, psychologically denied,
neglected, ignored, by the very people, all of them, whose business
is the uncovering and rectification of such unconscious falsification
by unintentionally turning a blind eye. It is an old tenet of criminal
justice that ignorance of the law is no protection from punishment;
conversely, however, the most intimate knowledge of the law does
make an offence against it seem the graver – and who could have a
clearer knowledge of the psychic laws involved in this collective
cover-up than the very perpetrators, united in quasi-political
loyalty? Watergate has nothing on it; at least, it wasn't torture and
the legitimization of torture that was concealed.

Secondly, in a phoney profession above all others, dog – as we
have had occasion to remark before – does not eat dog, not even if
the dog is Freud. No more depressing spotlight could be thrown,
not on human nature, but on human artificiality. The ethical
artefact of Freud's memorandum, its glibly resolved ambiguity, the
professional ease with which a palpably wriggling conscience is
silenced, are a warning to every phoney professional on this globe:
the phonier his profession, the more he will eventually need its
support, as distinct from the support of his own thoughts and his
own basic, natural decency.

Thirdly, and most feeling-provoking as well as thought-
provoking from the standpoint of our large-scale argument, there
is the actual object of this phoney profession's criticisms at that
particular stage – a traumatic stage – in the history of society: the
war neurotic. It did not even strike a Freud in this morally crucial
situation that his, or Wagner-Jauregg's, concept of neurosis was

entirely determined by the precepts of his society and, more important, his law-givers at that juncture in man's struggle to cope with,
and indeed extinguish, life. It did not strike him that according to
his own analytic insights, it would have been the easiest thing in the
psychological world to turn the tables on the psychiatric law-givers
and neurosis-givers, to declare those who had their inhibitions
about the business of killing normal, and those who accepted, even
enthused about, killing more abnormal than neurotics: successful
warfare is impossible without a stable basis of collective psychosis,
and I am merely going by Freud's discoveries, though not by his
words.

It is gradually dawning upon us, then, that the phoney professions do not only need an object for destructive criticism; they need
the easiest possible object, ideally one that cannot put up a fight –
one about which their society also holds a bad opinion and is thus
not likely to defend against them: only in this way can they ensure
their society's sustained esteem, without which they would be
nothing. In that sense, every society is responsible for its phoney
professions and has nothing to complain about, except that
'society' is a facile abstraction, a concept used with particular
pleasure and relief the way we have just used it – to escape the need
to blame individuals, particularly when it is difficult to find the
individuals to blame. But whether we find them or not, they are
there – countless individuals whose very guilt is, ultimately, their
own de-individualization, their rallying behind a collective idea,
attitude, purpose, practice, *modus vivendi*, which makes it difficult
to distinguish between them and so to find them, unless there is one
individual on top, a 'leader', who has the talent to bring out the
worst in all of them, and the worst is what they have in common:
when we hear of 'unity of purpose', we know that somebody is
going to suffer, be the unity religious, political, ethical, or indeed
aesthetic.

There is no substitute for the rebel, especially if he doesn't
emerge as a leader in his turn. Freud's single lasting moral mistake
was that under the pressure his phoney profession imposed upon
him, he formed a school in order to gain collective justification and
ensure the earliest possible esteem. Schoenberg, in a comparable
situation of initial loneliness, *didn't*: his pupils did. He did not even
teach his 'method of composing with twelve tones unrelated to
each other' the way Freud taught his psychoanalytic method – but

his pupils learnt it nevertheless. But then as a composer, Schoenberg's was not a phoney profession. He needed no victims – though
as we shall see,* as a teacher, he at least partook of phoney professionalism.

(v) The Teacher

If the psychoanalyst is related to the politician, the teacher – my last
phoney profession, though nowise the last the reader will be able to
think of – is related to the psychoanalyst, only he is not as well paid,
unless he, too, enjoys a private practice and is able to command his
fees. The teacher is, of course, considered an absolute necessity, as is
the psychoanalyst in certain American circles. The comparison is
not shallowly jocular: since the need for the psychoanalyst is
sociologically limited, we are in a position to observe that it doesn't
really exist – not to the extent to which it manifests itself in the
'Therapeutic State' anyway: I knew a distinguished American musician who wouldn't travel without his psychoanalyst.

The absolute need for the teacher, on the other hand, is not
sociologically limited, or at any rate far less so – whence it is far less
easy to recognize that in many circumstances, if not in most, the
teacher isn't really necessary, and may even be undesirable, harmful:
as every developed mind eventually realizes, self-education is the
only education which ultimately counts, beyond well-definable
preliminary stages with which we are not here concerned, for we are
thinking in terms not of teaching children, but of teaching minds
that have reached a measure of adult individuality. At that stage, too,
the teacher's influence can be entirely beneficial, if he rigorously
confines himself to stimulating self-education – in which case,
however, the title 'teacher' is a misnomer. In view of the effect which
language in general, and names in particular, have on human
thought (especially thoughtless thought, which depends on language altogether for doing the job of thinking), one might indeed
think of the possibility of introducing the profession of 'stimulator':
the feeble-minded question, 'Who did you study with?' would have
to be replaced by the more obviously half-empty 'Who were you
stimulated by?' and the frequently proud answer, invariably issuing
forth from the mouths of mediocrities, would have to be less proud.

---

*See p. 74.

Again, we are not thinking in terms of the teaching of special skills, though even in this area the necessity for teaching is vastly overestimated. Skills which are at the service of an expressive will, in particular, are often self-taught with brilliant success, even from childhood onwards. Instrumental technique is a prominent example: many are the outstanding instrumentalists who have not had an identifiable teacher, though it is true that any teacher that may have crossed a master's path in his youth is, at times, carefully concealed: some outstanding talents are as proud of their self-education as all mediocrities are of their teachers, if these are at all noteworthy.

In any case, the teacher's essential superfluity would only aggravate his phoniness; it wouldn't establish it, and the very esteem in which, by definition, we require him to be held in his society makes the task of showing, to that selfsame society, how well one could do without him, a cumbersome if not an impossible one. But in one respect which is definable with crystal-clarity, the unsolvable problems he creates can easily be shown to be worse, at once more acute and more lasting, than the problems with which the psychoanalyst burdens the voluntary and involuntary victims of his self-sustaining criticisms.

The teacher's patient is the student. And just as the typical psychoanalyst is dishonest about the educational influence he has on the patient, so the typical teacher is dishonest about the fact that he reduces the student's role to that of a patient. At the same time, the analyst has this to be said in his comparative favour, at any rate the orthodox Freudian analyst – that he regards it as his sacred duty to analyse and thus resolve the so-called transference situation, in which the patient has transformed his analyst into his parent, and his neurotic symptoms, maybe, into this unreal relationship: it is only when the patient's 'positive' and 'negative' transference (love and hate) evaporate by being brought down to earth and up to reality that, in theory at least, the analysis can be regarded as successfully concluded, that – ideally, at least – the analyst gets rid of the patient *pari passu* with the patient getting rid of the analyst. One of the classical, first-generation analysts, Karl Abraham, used to say that he knew he had succeeded in completing an analysis when the patient in question did not send him any picture postcards from his holidays.

The self-respecting teacher, on the other hand, wants and/or gets picture postcards all his life, or rather, all the student's life, and it is in this respect that the unsolvable problems he creates, not for himself but for his 'material', the student, are worse than the psychoanalyst, in that he first produces a transference situation and then refuses to make any attempt to resolve it: no wonder the mediocre, eternal student will always tell you who his teachers were and are – though current teachers are often kept a secret until they are past, when they turn into propaganda.

The official or unofficial student thus has a critic attached to him who accompanies him, quite often, throughout life. On the highest possible level of attainment, both on the student's and the teacher's part, a magnificent extreme example of such a chronic transference situation was Berg's and Webern's relationship to Schoenberg: they were his perpetual children, despite their sovereign gifts, sensitive to his criticisms, and anxious to gain his fatherly approval, as if they had never passed the age of six. In his defence, however, it can be pointed out that they needed him more than he needed them – that he did not, psychologically, *need* to criticize them at all. But criticize he did, and inasmuch as he created problems for them which he and they failed to solve, he fulfilled, as a teacher, the function of a phoney professional, however unphoney his professionalism as a composer.

That he did create problems for them is, admittedly, no more than a hypothesis – but right hypotheses are better than wrong facts, and wrong facts are less easily spotted than wrong hypotheses: in this disillusioned age, people are hypnotized by the 'factual approach' as such.

For one thing, I suggest that Webern's almost self-denying obsession with dodecaphonic structuralization, his 'exaggeration of everything new I find' (as Schoenberg once privately put it) was not, altogether, a creative blessing, and that more would have emerged, more that was less limited or – dare I say so? – inhibited emotionally if he had not projected his musical superego on to Schoenberg to an extent which made the master's own, self-critical conscience seem downright permissive in comparison. This, I concede, is not much more than theorizing, though one or the other reader who is closely acquainted with both Webern's and Schoenberg's music might come to agree that there is some considerable practical evidence to support my theory.

My case about Berg the problem-laden, overgrown child-student is, in any case, far more concrete and can be demonstrated in weighty detail. What I am suggesting is that as a creative character, Berg never was a twelve-tone composer and, *pace* his impressive output, would have been better off without his burning need to follow Papa, whatever the cost in terms of creative substance. It is not only that his craving for overt tonality was immeasurably deeper even than Papa's own – who at least succeeded in suppressing it for the greater part of his so-called 'classical' twelve-tone period, when he was still teaching himself the method as Beethoven was teaching himself string-quartet writing in the six quartets of Op. 18 (two of human history's greatest self-educators in all conscience!). Tonality and dodecaphony have, after all, proved combinable; in fact I have tried to show that tonality is but a species of serial technique, the tone-row being the triad, and the only difference being that the triad is there before the act of composition starts.

No, Berg's unconfessed aversion to twelve-tone technique is far more deep-seated than that and produces a purely nominal (but none the less eager) adherence to the technique which, again and again, stifles his natural style, or what clearly would have been his natural style if he had been left – or rather, if he had left himself! – to his natural devices. It is for this reason that many years ago, with all due respect, I included him amongst a category of composers which, I am proud to report to posterity, I was the first to discover – the *dodecaphoneys* – for he did not really write a single genuine twelve-tone piece in his life, one that stood the test of aural (as distinct from purely visual) recognizability and *qua* serial music, *meaning* – simply that.

In the Lyric Suite, at least, he swerves to and fro between dutiful (albeit meaningless) twelve-tone technique and so-called 'free atonality' – or, as I should describe it, not so free* demi-semi-tonality. But in *Lulu* (which, together with the Chamber Concerto, remains his greatest music notwithstanding its technical contortions), in order to follow (unspoken) parental command, he allowed himself a degree of dodecaphonic self-delusion which would have made him certifiable if he had evinced it in virtually any area outside modern music. But inside modern music, nobody noticed anything

---

*For a discussion of the concept of 'freedom' when applied to musical form, style and technique, see pp. 136ff.

amiss, neither the composer himself upon re-inspection, nor those to whom he explained the opera's technique in loving detail, accomplished musicians some of them. What I demonstrated at the time was that the subordinate tone-rows which Berg derived from his basic set were sheer, inadvertent humbug – that aurally, they meant nothing in terms of derivation, of unity with the primary row: in order to extend his range of expression which, he felt, was constricted by Papa's (self-)commandment of a single row, and in order to honour the single row while at the same time multiplying it, he played a purely numerical or numerological game with the father-row, giving birth to daughter-rows which were musically illegitimate: if, out of a given series of twelve different notes, you take every n^{th} in order to form a new series, nothing has happened aurally, musically, because you simply don't hear that way (unless, possibly, you are totally unmusical, yet cursed with perfect pitch like a dog). You don't count notes when you hear notes; you listen to their relations.

That a mind of Berg's intellect and ear should have been able to cheat himself across the very elements of musical perception shows the extent of his musico-moral disintegration under the weight of the problem with which Schoenberg had unwittingly loaded him, and which had remained duly unsolved. That, nevertheless, he achieved a work of the magnitude of *Lulu* or the Chamber Concerto proves the stature of his own creative mind and makes the question the more tempting: what would have happened without Papa's twelve-tone technique, though with his stimulation? At the very least, an enormous amount of obsessional energy would have been saved – and though Berg may have had to maintain a certain level of obsessionalism, there are more musical ways of being obsessional, and even intenser, more personal, and yet more substantial creativity would, in my opinion, have ensued: there is no way in which preoccupation with rubbish (his serial derivations) can be regarded as useful, helpful, or excused.

If such can be the effect of teaching in this historic situation, on a plane where angels (geniuses, extreme talents) tread with assurance, what is likely to happen on lower levels, to people who, condemned to be students or pupils for life, do not have the strength of personality, the clarity of purpose, the sheer creative will of an Alban Berg? To people that are the victims of more ruthless, less gifted teachers, who depend for their own lives on the lovingly critical mutilation of their pupils, on whom it is all the more incumbent, psychologically, to know better if the pupil is exceptionally gifted, likely to outshine the master at the first opportunity? Not everybody is a Schoenberg who, relatively early on, introduced his hefty volume on *Harmony** with the sentence, 'This book I have learnt from my pupils.'

I know what happens because I have been there: I am not devising my theories about the phoney profession of teaching in my armchair, I mean my beach-chair. In the course of my teaching years, I have become the most passionate anti-teacher teacher that has ever walked the earth; there aren't all that many of us, anyway. I have seen the depersonalizing effects of 'great' teaching, the evils of the teacher's altruism: the more good he is doing, the worse – the more is he imposing his personality and projecting his problems. It is even arguable – I throw this out as a logical possibility, not as a party-political statement, for I have no party – that the greatest teacher we know of has done more harm, depersonalized more lastingly, posthumously, than any other teacher, is innocently guilty of major crimes against humanity committed in his name – Jesus Christ. He would not have approved of the crimes – but they couldn't have been committed without his having depersonalized countless generations of disciples, and invented problems for them. The witch-pricker, after all, was one of those disciples, and with a little research, one could conceivably find that Jesus of Nazareth was the first true phoney professional in the history of mankind, and the first all-out critic too. Rabbis before him, at any rate, tended to be a little more modest in their aims.

But my case about the teacher stands without our having to pull Christ into it – as does the link between teacher and critic which, in its way, is as strong as that between psychoanalyst and teacher: all three of them, in fact, know precisely what's good for you, whether you like it or not. At the same time, the relation between teacher and critic is a little more specific than that; the only reason why it may not be obvious to any dispassionate observer is that the teacher does not address himself to an audience, so that you don't know precisely what is going on, whereas the critic addresses you.

However, this difference is not without exception, and as soon as we get hold of such an exception, we may find it difficult, on the contrary, exactly to distinguish between teacher and critic or their

---

*Harmonielehre, Vienna, 1911.

functions, professed or actual. The most drastic exception is not normal class teaching: there is an audience there, to be sure, but it is a student audience, and every listener is as much the object of the teacher's criticisms as he is a third party, an onlooker. It is a special kind of class that offers the closest possible parallel to the critical situation – the master class, which nowadays, when it has even been transferred to television, enjoys a wider audience upon occasion than any critic can hope for.

But even the television-less master class contains an ever-changing majority of third-party listeners who, at any given moment, are audience rather than objects of criticism. I think I should not have been able to criticize, with sufficient clarity, the situation paralleling that of music criticism which obtains in a master class if I had not myself conducted a particular type of master class on two occasions – a joint master class. In a normal master class, as a teacher, you are too involved in your own phoney activities to be able to spare a thought, a glance, for what is actually happening, as opposed to what you want to happen, and what the particular master-student you are concerned with is or isn't doing in response to your masterly advice – not to speak of your preoccupation with the audience, to whom you are, at the same time, addressing yourself as if you were giving a public lecture, watching facial reactions in case there seems to be any need to reiterate or clarify. But when you conduct a joint master class with another teacher, there are stretches where *you* are the audience – conscious, at the same time, that what you are listening to and watching is, *mutatis mutandis*, your own performance.

My experience of those two master classes could not possibly have been coloured by any impression of specific inadequacies on the part of my co-teachers; the reader will readily agree that one could not have wished for more admirable, more intrinsically musical, more articulate educators: one, at the Summer School of Music in Dartington, was its director, Sir William Glock; the other, at the Britten–Pears School for Advanced Musical Studies at The Maltings in Snape, was its own director, Peter Pears. With William Glock, I was in charge of a class that concerned itself with the problematic field of chamber music for piano and strings:* he

---

*In my opinion, in the whole of musical history (since the introduction of the piano), there are only six works which altogether overcome the problem of blend

concentrated on the pianists, I on the string players. With Peter Pears, I conducted a master class for singers – in oratorio arias and ensembles with obbligato instruments. His was an original idea: he suggested that he would concentrate on the instrumental side, and that I should devote my attention to the singers. Thereby, specialism would be avoided, technical preoccupations excluded, and sheer musicality would reign, since he didn't know much about instrumental technique, and I didn't know much about vocal technique. I was most enthusiastic – until it came to it.

When it did, he gravitated towards the singers, I, as a result towards the instrumentalists. Before we knew where we were, a situation had established itself that closely resembled the situation at Dartington which had made me think sceptically in the first place: here we were, my partner and I, with more than an eye on the audience and with insufficient thought for the performing student's psychological state, using him as material for our public lectures even when, ostensibly, we were addressing him rather than the audience. Like music critics, especially good critics who have something musical to say, we tactlessly divulged what should be soul-saving secrets (a case here for white discretion!) to all too eager eavesdroppers, turning them into our addressees. Each of us, no doubt, reserved his state of shock for the stage when the other one was committing the indiscretion; when we spoke ourselves, we could not be deflected from the importance of what we had to say.

Not to begin with, anyway. At The Maltings, both my partner and I soon began to show signs of guilty reaction. Peter Pears, that is, started murmuring to the singers, and I accompanied the instru-mentalists' performance with an economical running commentary close to their ears. The artists' gratitude was immediate; the audi-ence was less grateful.

Let it not be thought, however, that the absence of an audience necessarily improves the teacher's role, reduces the problems he devises for the pupil and the destructive effect of his criticisms: few are the teachers who can survive without their being their own

---

and balance posed by the combination of the piano with more than one stringed solo instrument. Mozart's two piano quartets overcome it without, as it were, noticing it, though he would have to admit that in the E flat Quartet, he made textural things relatively easy for himself by devising the work as a mini-piano-concerto. Schubert's and Mendelssohn's piano trios, two each, overcome the problem with ultra-sensitive textures which, *qua* textures, are wholly innovatory.

admiring audience, their own real addressees. Many are even doing the student a favour by letting him listen – with incomplete under-standing, needless to add, for God has decreed that the teacher's is the ultimate wisdom, the student's the ultimate inadequacy, which is why he will need the teacher's thoughts all his life. If, as not seldom happens, the blind thus succeeds in leading the blinded, the phoney profession has found its fulfilment.

5 Coda

At this point, the first question time as it were, since we are reaching the half-way stage of this book, three rhetorical questions can, I think, easily be anticipated. The first, if it were asked at a lecture, where question time usually (and fortunately) means answer time for the audience (so that the lecturer can hardly get in a question), would undoubtedly run something like this: 'If you're going on the way you do, you'll soon find that all professions, all occupations, are phoney – just as C. G. Jung found that everything was libido, and look where it got him: certainly not to a tenable theory of the mind. What sense is left in your thesis if the denotation of its central concept, "phoney professions", is so wide, its connotation so poverty-stricken?'

There are two answers. The first is that such a submission would not be true. Amongst the professions or vocations or callings which are without a trace of phoniness are those of the mathematician, the artist, and the pure scientist (not the one who created the problem of the hydrogen bomb, nor the one who created the problem of electro-convulsive therapy*). It is, clearly, for a reason which is not far removed from our own reasoning that Arthur Schopenhauer conceived this beautiful thought:†

> Corresponding to the purely intellectual life of the individual, there is the very same life of the whole of mankind, whose actual life also lies in the will. This purely intellectual life of mankind consists in the widening of knowledge through the sciences and the development of the arts. Down the ages and centuries, they both continue slowly

---

*Ugo Cerletti. He came to regret his discovery. Through the application of a general anaesthetic, one part of the problem – torture – has been removed, but the two other parts, never owned-up to, remain – possible loss of memory and possible change of personality, the latter arguably a fate worse than death.
†(See Appendix Note 2. Ed.)

while, contributing to them, the generations, one by one, hasten past them. Like an ethereal addition, a fragrant scent arising from fermentation, this intellectual life hovers over the worldly bustle, over the real life of the peoples which is led by the will; and alongside of the history of the world there goes, guiltless and unstained by blood, the history of philosophy, of science, and the arts.

The second answer is that I do not deny a spectrum, a scale of phoniness, and far from damaging my thesis, a comprehensive investigation into the type and degree of other professions would strongly support it. Part of medicine itself, for instance, is phoney – with its parental secret language which criticizes and degrades the patient, and its creation of therapeutic problems if not indeed of hospitals which are run for the doctors and nurses rather than for the patients, whose own interests would best be served, a small number of emergencies apart, if they could stay at home. But there are other parts of medicine which are absolutely free from phoney professionalism. All I have done in this section is to concentrate on one end of the scale, where the profession of criticism is securely installed.

The next rhetorical question would run parallel to the first: virtually all human activity includes criticism if the mind is involved at all, so why single out the phoney professions as particularly, and noxiously, critical? And my answer runs parallel to my last answer, too: a scale of critical involvement is not denied, but at the end of the scale on which I have been concentrating, criticism appears, at best, at its most useless, and at worst at its most destructive.

Thirdly, I should thus be challenged: 'The majority of us, your audience, are, one way or another, members of phoney professions, and conscientious members at that. What do you want us to do now? Go home and commit suicide?'

On the contrary, go out, back into your profession, and make a sustained, truthful, productive nuisance of yourself. If you are, as you say, a conscientious member of your profession, you are at least as highly esteemed as it is, especially by your colleagues. If, in addition, you are gifted, you are in an ideal position, professionally qualified and equipped, to assault the phoniness of your profession with all the considerable power at your disposal, to turn your destructive criticism towards an object, an idea, a conspiracy hiding behind a convention, which is worthy of destruction: don't forget the starting-point, the springboard of my thesis – the genius witch-pricker that never was, who would have attained one of the most towering achievements in the history of mankind. Even if, as is unlikely, you are not a genius, you might consider that fate, character and talent have placed you in a situation which enables you, if you will, to pursue one of the noblest causes, or rather anti-causes, that is open to man's imagination – the cause against outer authority, on which all phoney professions depend, and the cause for inner authority, for the authority of knowledge and ability, which is not a cause that has to be fought for, so long as obstacles in its way – phoney professional concepts – are removed. There is only one fruitful, peaceful type of rebellion – the knowing rebellion, which is the rebellion from within. All other revolutions make the world revolve, go round in circles; the rebellion of immediate insight makes it go upwards in a spiral.

At the stage we have now reached, the reader will not be surprised to learn that I speak with feeling; in fact, he will rightly accuse me of special pleading – of pleading the course of mental action which I decided upon for myself a long and, I hope, not altogether fruitless time ago. It wasn't, to begin with, a clear-cut decision; instinctive aversion to all varieties of moralization and to all instinctive acceptance of professional rules of conduct, of authority *qua* authority, preceded it – from the moment I was flung out of my first high school. I then suspected what has meanwhile been scientifically, and alarmingly, confirmed – that, in Anthony Storr's words,★ 'the human tendency to obey authority was much stronger than the equally human tendency to compassion'. That this is a scientific conclusion is evidenced by the, by now, widely known experiments on which it is based – those by S. Milgram† who, again in Storr's words:‡

devised a situation in which normal American students believed that they were studying the effect of punishment upon learning. To this end they were required to administer electric shocks to a fellow subject each time he made a mistake in a simple learning task. Moreover, they were required to increase the severity of the shock after

---

★*Human Destructiveness*, London, 1972, p. 29.
†'Behavioral Study of Obedience', *Journal of Abnormal and Social Psychology*, vol. 67, no. 4, 1963, pp. 371–8. 'Some Conditions of Obedience and Disobedience to Authority', *Human Relations*, vol. 18, 1965, pp. 57–76.
‡op. cit.

each mistake . . . these normal students would continue to give what they genuinely believed to be painful, or even potentially lethal, shocks to their fellows, in spite of warnings marked on the apparatus, simply because they were urged to by the experimenter.

I should, in my turn, urge the reader to consider that there are two levels of pure phoney professionalism here, one artificially induced and proudly presented to the psychological and sociological world, the other lamentably natural and, accordingly, utterly undetected by professional psychologists or indeed anybody else – for everybody else only too happily submits to the authority of professional psychologists. The piece of artificial phoney professionalism is the behaviour of the torturing students, who are satisfied that they are acting in accordance with professional requirements. But even more distressing is the wholly unconscious phoney professionalism of the experimenter himself – who, accepting the authority of well-established experimental psychology and psychiatry (and on the model, perhaps, of those controlled experiments on electro-shock in which patients are told they are given the treatment but aren't), is prepared, with a relaxed conscience, to treat actual people as his mere material for criticism, deceive them, and make at least a temporary mess of their psyche in the process.

Thousands and thousands of words have been written about these experiments which have been the subject of comment, respectful, admiring, awe-inspired, not only in books and specialist journals, but in the more ordinary press all over the place – yet I haven't seen a single word about this question of the experimenter's justification to undertake his experiment. It is not a complex intellectual question or a subtle moral point, a problem in which only the ethical pedant would be interested; it's a question of elementary human decency which has been ignored by the whole, would-be civilized world, intellectual and News-of-the-Worldly, under the influence of phoney professionalism. In fact, the *News of the World* never ceases to moralize; why did it not, for once, take up a simple moral point without the support of any moral authority, just because a single individual thought of it? But then, no single individual seems to have thought of it; they were all too little single as it were, too grateful for the opportunity for collective criticism of those subjects of the experiment, the obedient students, richly as they deserved it – but only in the context of a total recognition of the offences against humanity here committed.

As I have indicated, thoughts of this nature dawned upon me but gradually – but as a teenage violinist, with the help of the only teacher I acknowledge, Oskar Adler,* I soon recognized the bogus division between violin and viola and turned into a viola player at the same time: my first conscious act directed against phoney professionalism. From then onwards, my suspicions of professionalism of sundry kinds became ever clearer. Transplanted to England, I was advised by my seniors that it was unprofessional for a writer not to write in his mother-tongue, which confirmed my decision to write in English. And when I had taken full measure of what I thought were the horrors of music criticism, I plunged into that profession in order to fight the fraternity as a step-brother. No sooner had I become a musicologist (it was never I who called myself that, always others) than I started to try and clear the air in that scholarly world, and when I was recognized as a psychoanalytic writer, I turned my attention to the flawed concepts of that profession. I have mentioned my anti-educational activities as a teacher, and it is hardly necessary to explain why, as a very grown-up man, I became a professional broadcaster: by now, the urge to try and clean up phoney professions from within was approaching anti-missionary zeal. For close on ten years, however, I was a tolerably good boy in the broadcasting world – until I had achieved the necessary seniority and outer authority to make my voice felt, to make authoritative attempts to silence me impossible. Throughout my adult life, then, I have felt this intellectual passion – to save some little part of the world from the professional world-savers, if and when the world they were out to save was within reach of my professional competence, so that I could constructively join it in the first place. It is not for me to say how far, if at all, I am succeeding. I am content whenever any phoney professional agrees to think again and, maybe, use his talents towards the explosion of professional humbug. It is for reconsideration I am pleading – and this is the extent of my special plea. As the first half of what I hope are our joint (though not collective!) reflections closes, the reader may already have come to deem it possible that there are worse kinds of specialism.

---

*See p. 41.

Part II

CRITICISM

Man does not live by praise alone – which, as this book will show, may be a pity. In fact, much as he enjoys his own enthusiasm, he enjoys blame even more, and his favourite relaxation, once he has attained a measure of civilization, is to find things wrong with things – a salutary compulsion where things are wrong, a tragedy where, as not seldom in art, they aren't. One might go so far as to say that art is the only dimension of human activity where perfection is reached, yet art is the very field on which professional fault-finding concentrates; it is as if the last thing man could bear was perfection, or even imperfect greatness. There is good psychological reason to assume that we do not readily allow anybody to presume above his (our) station; a very unradical, psychoanalytic psychologist with a wellnigh unequalled breadth of vision went so far as to postulate a 'Polycrates complex' in all of us,★ the result of our need for punishment of both ourselves and those who, in our view, have the arrogance to aspire to the status of supermen. However that may be – and there is plenty of evidence to suggest that we find it difficult to tolerate the overdog – one thing is certain: there has not been a great artist in history who escaped violent criticism, whereas many a small artist did. Of course, such criticism need not always express itself actively; passive critical resistance, total neglect, can be at least as effective – as it was in the case of Jane Austen, whom the critics successfully ignored, a circumstance which must have intensified her diffidence about her literary status, costing her, in terms of psychic economy, a great deal of energy that might have been employed more fruitfully in a life that was cut short at the age of forty-two, even though her genius no doubt turned such misfortune to creative advantage.

★J. C. Flugel, *Men, Morals and Society*, London, 1945, pp. 151ff.

But outside the world of art, too, the urge to criticize – or, to put it more bluntly, the urge to loathe, hate, reject, never ceases. The statistically-minded may find it illuminating to chance upon any conversation as eavesdroppers – as I am doing on the beach where I am writing this book at moments of repose – and measure the proportion of negative criticism in which the participants indulge, whether they have much in common or not, and regardless of whether they are a duet or a more complex ensemble. Invariably, it will be found that finding things wrong with things covers more than fifty per cent of the total amount of intercommunication, at any rate in terms of time, if the conversationalists are not lovers, in which case you can't hear what they are saying anyway, and wouldn't – you being you – want to if you could.*

My reference to secret love and undisguised hate, or an impulse springing from hate, is neither flippant nor, in the context of the argument I am developing, faulty. Many are our secret love affairs, our impulses of one or the other kind of love about which we feel guilty. But of our hates we don't make any secret at all, unless there are practical, utilitarian reasons for doing so. If we go back to the individual's prototypical combination of love and hate, i.e. the Oedipus situation, or rather if he goes back to it in his thoughts and is able to penetrate his repressions to the extent of remembering that he wanted to sleep with his mother, he will not find it easy to tell other people about his infantile desires. But if he remembers that he hated his father, he will divulge the news without much embarrassment, guilty as he may have felt about his state of mind at the time.

The fact is that as a matter of inevitable psychological course, we moralize hate, while we do not necessarily moralize love: civilized man, unless he is a psychopath in whom not much of a conscience is detectable anyway, simply does not allow himself to hate without what he regards as good moral reason. The very circumstance that in childhood, hatred is accompanied by guilt reactions, by self-hatred, is introverted, ensures that good psychological care is

---

*Too heavily preoccupied with statistics? At least, it won't cost you anything, and the reward in terms of hard factual information will be instantaneous. In 1976, on the other hand, our Department of Transport spent £1.95 million on statistics, compared to £50,000 in 1974: that cost you quite a little, and the reward is obscure. Have you nothing better to spend your money on?

taken to place moral right on the side of all later hates, all destructions, the worst of which – wars, genocide – are perpetuated for moral reasons, while the perpetrators will keep a boring love affair a guilty secret. I hate because, but I don't always love because.

In psychoanalytic terms, spontaneous, conscious love is an ego function, whereas conscious hate necessarily involves the superego – the mind's critical agency. In more normal terms, therefore, and without any attempt at aphoristic exaggeration, it can be said that civilized hate is a function of one or the other type of criticism – that it doesn't allow itself expression, even consciousness, without appearing in the guise of such a function. If this simple train of thought has any validity at all, its realistic implications are shattering, the possibilities of *self-righteous* hate unlimited: there isn't any other, and there is a lot of hate. If you can't lick it, join it – this is the attitude of man's conscience towards his aggression.

Ever since technology has made possible mass killing on an even wider scale than mass communication, while, on the other hand, man is beginning to see through some of the moralizations of hatred (since no large-scale agreement on morals is left anyhow), the problem of destructiveness has moved into the centre of psychological, sociological, religious, and even political attention: the politicians always come last and least, being led by those whom they are paid for leading. If the original Freudian revolution, which dominated the advanced intellectual life of the first half of our century, concentrated on sex, especially in innocent childhood, the secondary Freudian revolution (yes, that can be traced back to him, too!) swerved over to the need to kill and die, again with primary attention to the infant's savagery. Our current preoccupation with human destructiveness, that is (Anthony Storr's afore-quoted book is, in fact, part of a series of 'Studies in the Dynamics of Persecution and Extermination'), was dramatically anticipated by Freud's revised instinct theory, which he postulated as early as 1920,[*] under the impact, in Erich Fromm's more recent view,[†] of the First World War: from now on, the life instinct (Eros) and the death instinct were going to be the mind's fundamental polarity, the death instinct being directed against the self in the first place, and also in the last, at death, but extraverted in between.

---

[*] *Beyond the Pleasure Principle.*
[†] *The Anatomy of Human Destructiveness*, London, 1974, pp. 439ff.

Whatever science will ultimately think of this postulate (over which the war of the theorists continues to rage unabated), there is no doubt that at least metaphorically – poetically, if you like – Freud got hold of one of the profoundest truths to which we are alive, even though his theory does little towards explaining the specifically human passion for the destruction of members of its own species; though dog does not eat dog, man eats man, literally so, even in modern times, and even though he may be a citizen of a country more developed than developing: in a speech before the Syrian National Assembly, General Mustafa T'Las, Syria's Minister of Defence, paid tribute to a war hero who had personally killed twenty-eight Israelis in the 'Yom Kippur' war:*

'He butchered three of them with an ax and decapitated them. In other words, instead of using a gun to kill them he took a hatchet to chop their heads off. He struggled face-to-face with one of them, and throwing down his ax managed to break his neck and devour his flesh in front of his comrades. This is a special case. Need I single it out to award him the Medal of the Republic? I will grant this medal to any soldier who succeeds in killing twenty-eight Jews, and I will cover him with appreciation for his bravery.'

It must be soberly realized that both the distinguished cannibal and His Excellency the Minister (as which, in all seriousness and with ultra-phoneydom, we should address him) were, respectively, acting and talking in a purely critical capacity; as Saul Bellow points out in the book on which I unleashed my own destructive criticism† – of which more in its proper place‡ – the Egyptian and Syrian leaders regard the foundation of the State of Israel as 'original sin',§ and there cannot be a more worthy object of criticism than that, even though incorporation has, in the past, happened as the result of more favourable, or at least more ambivalent criticism and, symbolically, is continuing thus to be practised amongst the most civilized – in the Roman Catholic ritual.¶

When I talked about the specifically human passion for destruction within the species, I exaggerated, but only just. There are one

---

*David Gutmann reporting in the *Middle East Review*, autumn 1975.
†See pp. 56ff.
‡See pp. 103ff.
§op. cit. p. 170.
¶Cf. Freud, *Totem and Taboo*, 1913.

or two types of non-humans that are human enough to kill each other – 'creatures which form clans or colonies in which individual members recognize one another by smell. Social insects such as bees, termites and ants will destroy any member of another colony which strays into their midst; and so will rats and other rodents. The biological reason for this is obscure . . .',★ but one anthropologist, Robert Bigelow, 'argues not only that primitive man lived in small groups which were indeed perpetually hostile to one another' and 'produces an impressive array of examples', including 'the few "stone-age" peoples surviving today in the remoter valleys of New Guinea.'† 'Dog does not eat dog', when metaphorically applied, not to a species, but – as by the erstwhile Music Critic of *The Times*‡ – to a group (such as music critics) within a species, would thus emerge as an amusing atavism, without much later intelligence to support it, for there is little reason to strengthen the implied view that since a music critic has to eat, he should eat musicians rather than critics. Like the rest of humanity, the critic doesn't quite know what to do with his aggression, but unlike most of the rest, he – like the soldier, the hangman, and the vet – is invested with the authority to kill if necessary; moreover, it is left to him to decide when it is necessary, and since he harbours this need to kill, the necessity often arises.

Whatever the answer to the grave problem of human destructiveness, then – whether it is a question of instinct, or of frustrations produced by early environment or, most likely, a bit of both – the fact remains that each human being, or each clan, has to find his or its own answer in psychological terms. The phoney professions, and the critics in particular, have succeeded in institutionalizing their answer: one way or another, they are all professionally destructive. But while the other phoney professions have merely moralized destructive criticism as part of their professional equipment, the professional critic has exalted it to the status of original virtue – with the result that 'to criticize' means to criticize unfavourably, unless the concept is specially qualified.

For let it not be said that throughout, we are developing a

★Storr, op. cit., p. 25.
†Storr, op. cit., p. 14; the reference is to R. Bigelow's *The Dawn Warriors*, Boston, 1969, London, 1970.
‡See my Preface, pp. 3–4.

one-sided picture of criticism, confining ourselves to its negative side and paying little heed to what is often piously known as 'constructive criticism', especially when it wants to hide some part of its aggression. It is not we who are developing the one-sided picture; it is critical and linguistic usage itself. Let us not stand on semantic ceremony: there is a palpable difference between what the dictionaries tell us 'criticism', 'to criticize' means and the sense in which the concept is used, misused, and abused.

When we say that somebody adopts an uncritical attitude towards something, we are not complaining about his lack of analytic discernment, his thoughtless reactions. They may, in fact, be exceedingly thoughtful, but if all these many thoughts are favourable, his response will still be branded as uncritical. Divested of all vaguely implied sophistication, which we should be hard put to define, we simply mean that the culprit hasn't found anything bad in his object of investigation: this is what makes him uncritical. Critical 'objectivity', a virtue sought after especially in historical research, is, in effect, measured solely in terms of the critic's ability to find something bad in something good: it is as simple, as crude, as self-righteously destructive as that. The critic in question is automatically assured favourable reviews of his piece of research; his peers will find that he has mastered the craft of detached scholarship, however intense his – in the circumstances, laudable – enthusiasm. No fellow critic will ask whether those bad things were found or invented – or, if they were found (and also if they weren't), whether they matter, and why.

The conspiracy of destructiveness is unassailable – except by such glaring, unscholarly, un-musicological amateurs as, say, a Richard Wagner, who was constitutionally incapable of finding all the bad things in the Beethoven quartets (which, however, he coached)* which the pioneer discoverer Joseph Kerman† unearthed by way of scrupulous critical destructiveness, so persuasively that there must be many who secretly wish that Professor Kerman might one day recompose the bad bits in order to let Beethoven shine unblemished in his glory which, admittedly, he deserved even from an unbiased point of view, whatever his shortcomings: after all, he was only

---

*Cosima Wagner's Diaries, in Geoffrey Skelton's translation. London, Collins, 1978, vol. I, p. 315. (See also pp. 96–7.)
†Author of The Beethoven Quartets, London, OUP, 1967.

human. Whereas the real critical point to make would be that he wasn't. But that wouldn't be criticism, for there is no criticism worth its acknowledged name without a critical situation being postulated – a crisis of thought produced by that destructiveness which the recipient of the criticism enthusiastically identifies with; for he, too, is in perpetual search of stable channels for his aggression – *ceteris paribus* even more so, in fact, than the critic or musicologist, who has this destructiveness built into his professional system.

Or the historian, if he deals with evaluation at all, within the musical world and without. Arthur Schopenhauer used to sneer at history as an intellectual discipline which, of its very nature, runs the continual risk of the *post hoc, ergo propter hoc* fallacy and, even amongst its most refined practitioners, cannot but fall victim, at least occasionally, to projecting causality not only on a mere succession of events, but also, it seems to me, on their correlation which, in reality, is causal only in that the events in question have a common cause rather than causing each other, as have night and day. But ever since the age of objectivity started, primarily in reaction to so-called romantic hero-worship, this new danger has, as a temptation, presented itself to the evaluating, the *critical* historian – to canalize his own destructiveness into a professional virtue and, inspired by the spirit of detachment, find fault especially where impeccability used to reign.

In the entire history of the western mind, one chief villain has emerged in the age of objectivity, for a variety of reasons, all of them easy to uncover – Richard Wagner. For one thing, as a person, he had always been felt to have presumed far above his station, to lack any trace of modesty or humility: no genius, perhaps, was so conscious of being a genius – as if there was anything wrong with that, with being conscious of the truth. Karlheinz Stockhausen, incidentally, may be another candidate for the job of supreme self-recognition, except that he may not be all that much of a genius.

For another thing, Wagner's music, like none other before or indeed after him, let what Freud called the dynamic unconscious, normally inaccessible, erupt with a clarity and indeed seductiveness which will always be likely to arouse as much resistance (to the listener's own unconscious) as its sheer power creates enthusiasm. Thirdly, heroic music is 'out' anyway: it isn't only the historical hero-worshipper who finds himself unwanted in and by our time, but also the artist who expresses an heroic concept.

But Wagner's music, at least, encounters more ambivalence than straightforward rejection, and while, among the upper strata of the musical intelligentsia, there are more rejectors than ever before, the Wagner operas continue to sell out all over the world as if nothing had happened. What has happened is that even amongst those who admire the music or else regard it with intense, extreme ambivalence, 'objective' destructiveness has been displaced on to, or made to concentrate on, the man, in order to make things psychologically easy for the observer, who can love the music and save his soul, as well as spending his aggression, by hating the man. Those who hate Wagner's music hate the man anyhow; and those who love or love-hate it, critical historians above all, find the possibilities offered by our century's new objectivity, its anti-hero-worship, a godsend.

As a result, the man has been destroyed by friend and foe and critical referee alike, and an objective picture has been created of his personality, by critic after critic, which is indistinguishable from the image of a phantom. It is not here suggested that there was nothing wrong with Wagner, nor is it suggested that there is nothing wrong with you and me. But you and I, luckily, can't compose like that, and so we are safe.

I had suspected for many years (and, so far as I remember, committed my suspicions to public print, but in any case bored all my friends with them) that the official picture we have of Wagner's character was a destructive delusion; I am not a cordial believer in biographies anyway, for I cannot see how people can know more about people they never knew than about people they do – and we have all experienced what a single person's picture of another person is like, avail itself though it may of other people's opinions. But not even at the very height of my persecution mania on Wagner's behalf would I have believed it possible that the job I had done inside myself as Wagner's unofficial picture restorer could be outdone by reality; reality would have to try jolly hard.

It did, in the shape of Cosima Wagner, and succeeded: for once, a biographer was to be trusted, because she was in the position of using herself as a forerunner of the tape recorder, with an unlimited amount of time and tape at her disposal. In 1976, that is to say, the complicated copyright difficulties which had long delayed the publication of Cosima Wagner's diaries had finally been overcome, and

the first volume, covering the years 1869–77, was published.★
Below, I am printing a translated extract from my very long review
which appeared in the *Frankfurter Allgemeine Zeitung* on 9 October
1976. It exposes, I submit, the unanimous destructive criticism of a
whole era – and, beyond that, the extent to which human destructiveness can successfully express itself by way of criticism without
anybody noticing anything amiss after the corpse has been
embalmed. If, aside from this demonstration, the reader suspects
that my review is submitted as a proposed model of anti-destructive,
reconstructive criticism, he is right:†

> Biography, it is not generally realized, is a form of torture – or can
> easily be, anyway: the helpless victim is at the biographer's mercy. And
> if the victim is dead in the first place, so much the worse for him: there
> is not even the law of libel to protect him. Other things being equal, the
> more biographies a man has had to suffer, the less remains of him.
> Since Wagner is one of the most-biographed individuals in the history
> of mankind, we should have suspected all along that he must have been
> tortured out of existence in the process – but no: the magic of the
> printed word transcends reason.
>
> However, now that Cosima's *Diaries* are, at last, accessible and the
> first volume is in fact available, at least to the German-reading public,
> we are coming to realize the errors of our thoughtless ways of learning.
>
> The book is a cultural sensation: this has to be said, without the
> slightest sensationalism. It has absolutely nothing to do with the
> Richard Wagner whom we think we know – nor do we have to depend
> all that much on Cosima's own impressions: day in, day out, she
> recorded what he said and did, and even if we ignore what she thought
> of it all, countless biographers stand condemned. The modern 'objec-
> tive' biographies are, of course, the worst – for to be 'objective' means
> to be able to find something bad.
>
> Let's face it: how many are there amongst us who can resist the urge
> to take revenge upon genius? Compared to the degradation of genius
> which we – the 'mature' scholars – compulsively practise, so-called
> adolescent hero-worship is a downright scientific search for reality –
> for it at least starts out from a piece of reality that overshadows
> everything else: the reality of greatness. Twenty-odd years ago, the
> psychoanalytic psychologist J. C. Flugel‡ discovered (or, as his adver-

‡*Men, Morals and Society*, London, 1945.

★Cosima Wagner, *Die Tagebücher*, vol. 1: 1869–77, ed. Martin Gregor-Dellin and
Dietrich Mack, Munich and Zurich, R. Piper & Co., 1976.
†(See Appendix Note 3. Ed.)

saries thought, invented) the 'Polycrates complex', which drives us –
in my own words – to find smallness in greatness: we do not readily
allow man to presume above his station, and if he is a demonstrable
genius, our only remaining hope is that as a person, a human being,
he was a nasty piece of work; nasty hope springs eternal.

Wagner, of course, made sure that nobody would miss his pre-
sumption – except Cosima. She was chronically in love with him – a
problem, this, for those psychologists who are fond of creating
problems which they can't solve, for nothing is as difficult to solve as
a pseudo-problem, whose reality one has to dream up in the first
place. But with her penetrating, clear-sighted intelligence, Liszt's
daughter goes with Wagner all the way and sends the Polycrates
complex to the devil – whence, after all, it came: she realizes that in
the world of thought, underestimation is original sin. There are only
few humans, intellectual saints all of them, who are without this sin,
and Cosima is one of them: her love, which helped her towards her
saintliness, may seem a problem to us, but for her it was a solution.

Nor need psychoanalytic theory worry. True, it postulates male
rather than female 'overestimation of the love object', but who says
that Cosima's estimate of Wagner was overestimation? Such would-
be scientific suspicions hide a begging of this question – whether a
towering genius can have been, at the same time, a charming, helpful,
human man: that, surely, would be too much of a good thing!

Thus we desperately cling to Wagner's weaknesses, such as his
anti-Semitism (which did not, of course, apply to the Jews he liked)
or his anti-French posture – both of which turn out to be so silly and
boring, such thoughtless generalizations of unpleasant personal
experiences (e.g. unfavourable criticisms), that they don't even cause
the present writer, a pretty conscious Jew, more than a yawn. They
are, in fact, out of character – Wagner's otherwise extremely well-
integrated character – and obtrude, like lifeless desert islands, from
the boiling sea of his ever restless imagination.

Cosima, then, not only estimates Wagner realistically, i.e. simply
as a genius (if 'simply' is the word), but presents him as an eminently
human being. She doesn't *say* that his art apart, he is quite a person;
she *shows* him to have been one.

Phantasy without realistic thought is nothing – psychosis at most.
Once one has recovered from the shock that Wagner was not a
revolting man at all (and it will take a long time for this pathogenous
fantasy to die), one is struck by the yet more important fact that his
conceptual thinking was just as alert, as sleepless, as his musical
thinking. Perhaps one shouldn't be surprised – but the fact remains
that amongst creative musicians, such double intellects are exceptional: one or two romantics (not forgetting Hans Pfitzner) and

Schoenberg seem to have been the only composers whose conceptual intellect equalled Wagner's. At the same time, Wagner was the only one amongst them who, in his own musical world, suffered under conceptual – extra-musical – loneliness: 'Would that I were not a musician: what a category of uneducated human beings into which this wretched note-scribbling has thrown me!'

Cosima noted down his thoughts with untiring conscientiousness – and they poured forth from breakfast until late at night (whenever he didn't compose or write) – without much regard for the 'normal' worries of everyday life. What is equally astonishing is that he never permitted himself to formulate anything he hadn't thought out, to say anything he hadn't clearly formulated within. For example, he explained Schopenhauer's concept of the 'will' to her in a few clear words whose historical location one would never have guessed, for they seem to teem with Freudian insight and are marked by what we think is twentieth-century concision: '". . . the urge, first to live, then to understand, and eventually to destroy. [Freud's life and death instincts!] Remorse – which is our knowledge that something lives in us that is much more powerful than our idea of evil"': the Freudian unconscious and the conflicts to which it gives rise. Incidentally, the childish view that Wagner was one of the roots of Nazism has to face this psychological warning of Wagner's – that impossible evil is possible. Mind you, his (i.e. Schopenhauer's) pessimistic verdict on man's potential immorality was, on another occasion, thrown into the shade by Wagner's remark to Cosima – and I am translating literally – that people 'are yet more stupid than they are more evil': the second comparative establishes the link with Schopenhauer, in that it implies that they are more evil than we (and they) think.

The editors of the book emphasize in their preface that the *Diaries* are 'a faithful protocol of the spirit of the times, which could not conceivably have been less distorted'. Well, the reader will perhaps appreciate my reaction when I say, with respect, that the editors are here committing a literary crime which the Austrian wit and cultural historian Egon Fridell used to describe as 'manslaughter' – an insult intended as a compliment. For it should be obvious, even from the couple of quotations I have submitted, that inasmuch as Cosima's diary entries concentrate on Wagner's thoughts, they are almost uncannily untimely, timeless, prophetic: they sound as new, as recent, as does his music, and so remind us of Goethe's penetrating thought in his *Elective Affinities*: 'Invariably, the greatest minds are linked with their century through weakness'; which means that you can't have both – their strengths and the spirit of their times. And not unnaturally, Cosima limited her record, on the whole, to Wagner's greatness (if you can call that a limitation).

The central reason, however, why this is by far the most important book about Wagner ever is that it shows, quite unambiguously, how wrong all the other books go when they describe his attitude to music in general, and to his own creations in particular; and it has to be added that the most thoughtful books are the worst, because they are the most inventive. That is to say, the musician whom we think we know as the tempter, the seducer, if not the rapist *par excellence,* whose sole aim was to overpower the public, largely with the black magic of his orchestrations – a pure devil who did not even divine what pure music was about. And now listen to the composer's own relevant reflections: 'I get nothing out of the performances of my works except trouble and worry, and the satisfaction of nothing going wrong – no other impression, not any longer. My stuff only gives me joy until the stage of the first ink version of the score, when the original nebulous, pencilled thought suddenly stands clearly and distinctly before me. The instrumentation, however, is too much of this world . . . Why should I be pleased that the things I wrote twenty years ago are taken note of – now that I am much further ahead? Why should I make one step forward and two back? I have been shaken too violently for that.' The year is 1871, seven years before the composition of *Parsifal* was started – the opera which has become the A and O of sensuous, hypnotic instrumentation. For the rest, the difference between Wagner's spirit and the spirit of his times is once again thrown into relief here – for it is an eminently future spirit whom his rhetorical question, 'Why should I be pleased . . .' anticipates, wellnigh verbatim: I have it from an ear-witness, Egon Wellesz, that Schoenberg asked this very question after the long-delayed, highly successful first performance of *Gurrelieder* on 13 February, 1913 – when, in the artists' room, people congratulated him on the astonishing reception.

As for the music of other great composers, especially Bach, Mozart and, of course, Beethoven, we find countless observations whose analytic profundity has absolutely nothing to do with the style of musicography in Wagner's time: in view of his downright musicological mind, we become guiltily aware of the fact that it wasn't the twentieth century that has discovered what we tend to regard as musical analysis proper. Even when he talked about Beethoven as his own predecessor, Wagner adopted the kind of factual approach which we possessively consider our own time's alone: 'In the evening, we continued to read [Goethe's] *Wilhelm Meister*: great joy. We then came to talk about Beethoven, and Richard said: "The only time when Beethoven was not concise was in the finale of the great B flat Sonata. Your father alone can play this movement, and when he does it is his virtuosity I enjoy, much more than the music itself. Concision seems to be the secret of music; when the melody stops and is supposed to be replaced by some sort of work, the effect stops. Beethoven was the first to turn everything into melody, the first to have shown how one and the same theme gives rise to ever new themes, each an autonomous entity.''' Anticipated here are, again, the insights of Schoenberg and his school, one of whose members (Erwin Stein) described Beethoven as the first musical thinker – just because of his subterranean monothematicism.

At the same time, Wagner only accepted demonstrable predecessors; not for him any vague discoveries of historical precedent: 'When I came home, I found Professor Nietzsche and his friend, Mr Rohde, also a philologian; they had already announced themselves yesterday. Conversation – cheerfully serious. In the evening, Professor Nietzsche read us his lecture on "The Greek Music Drama", to which title Richard took exception, giving reasons for his reproof. But the lecture is beautiful and shows that Nietzsche has really felt, experienced Greek art.' Cosima's exclusive concentration on Richard does, however, produce one serious disadvantage: we hear far too little about one or two other geniuses of Wagner's acquaintance, such as Nietzsche himself, or indeed Brahms. Again and again, we read that Nietzsche had been to visit – without being allowed a glimpse of what he said.

A spotlight, finally, on Wagner the man we don't know – and I don't mean the family man, for within the family circle, it is often easier to be, or appear, human, especially if you have Cosima there to report on you. No, let us leave personal relations as well as relatives out of it: 'Yesterday [on 10 February, 1869] Richard told me that he was stopped, on the Reuss Bridge, by a timpanist who identified himself as one of the musicians that played in Richard's Zurich concerts in 1859, and who told him that the entire Zurich orchestra was full of gratitude to Richard: they are now receiving the treatment Richard had, at the time, demanded for them from the members of the Musical Society, to wit, a firm, regular salary and permanent employment. They now have a personnel of 32 players who are employed summer and winter. Richard asked the timpanist to convey his greetings to the gentlemen of the committee – as well as the message that they could have taken this measure a little earlier.'

The editors of the book have, on the whole, done a first-rate job, conscientious almost throughout: there are but a few mistakes in the index of names, such as occur in any volume of comparable size. But while the chronological table is wonderfully planned and, of course, most welcome, it is quite often amateurishly incomplete: one has to ask oneself whether pressure of time necessitated editorial dependence on outside help which, in the event, has proved inadequate. We are

told about Lord Byron's and Bruckner's birth in 1824, for instance,
but not about Smetana's (an early Wagnerian's!) – whose death
remains unrecorded too, with the result that 1884, the year after
Wagner's death, is not listed at all. Again, Schoenberg and Stravinsky
are allowed to be born, but poor old Bartók isn't: in his year of birth,
we only learn about Dostoevsky's death and Picasso's birth. Webern's
birth in the year of Wagner's death remains unmentioned – and the
fact that in 1885, Daimler invented the automobile with combustion
engine is, perhaps, a little less important for the world in which this
book moves than Alban Berg's birth in the same year. Brecht's birth,
on the other hand, is not forgotten – while Hindemith is ignored
altogether.

But what the reader of this article wants to know in the first place is
whether he should read the book when Geoffrey Skelton's English
translation is completed and becomes available. Never in my writing
life have I recommended biographical material so whole-heartedly, so
whole-mindedly.

While only a thorough perusal of the entire mammoth volume
can give a complete picture of the historico-critical character assas-
sination, both personal and artistic, to which Wagner had been
subjected until, at long last, he was allowed informally to speak for
himself, the reader has now seen quite enough evidence to realize
that we do not need the deliberate falsifications of history of which
Nazi historians and Marxist historians alike have been so sensa-
tionally guilty in our century in order to achieve, under the welcome leadership of semi-detached historiography, collectively
accepted distortions of the truth which serve no political aim, but
the seemingly more modest purpose of legitimized, authorized
instinctual gratification. Seemingly more modest, for in psychological fact, political aims are equally modest in that they follow the
same purpose, however complex the rationalizing superstructure of
thought about national (or, for that matter, international) welfare
may be – and other things being equal, the more political aims
unite, the more exclusively instinctual the satisfaction they offer,
because it is only primitiveness that we all have in common and
love to see collectively justified, placed firmly above board.

As for the subsidiary, didactic intention behind my extended
self-quotation, the reader, I dare say, is about to lose his patience
which, for the duration of the present section, has been sorely tried:
if your own critical behaviour is all that much of a model, he will
burst out, and if human destructiveness is, as you reiterate, the

original evil behind criticism, what about your own review of Saul Bellow's *To Jerusalem and Back*,★ which you seem to have quoted with such pride or, as I would call it, with obnoxious self-satisfaction? Can there be anything more destructive than that? Wasn't this what the Literary Editor of the *Guardian* was concerned about, and yet you criticize him instead of on your own premises, criticizing yourself?

It is quite true that this review is the most aggressive and indeed the most destructive piece I have written in years. But the basic question is, *what does it destroy?* In principle, I put it to the no longer gentle reader, the very same thing which my review of Cosima Wagner's *Diaries* helps to destroy, i.e. critical destructiveness itself. In the case of Cosima's book, she (not to speak of Wagner himself) had done all the important work – which I merely had to stress and interpret. In the case of Saul Bellow's, his inane if playful assault on one of the greatest works of art which, at the same time, is still underrated just because it is played too often and too superficially, and heard too often and too superficially. There are, in short, plenty of people who think about the Mendelssohn Violin Concerto as Saul Bellow does, and think they have an aesthetic right to do so – because, as we have shown, there is no destructive thought that does not deem itself right. When they see what they think, or dimly feel, confirmed by what they wrongly regard as Saul Bellow's authority – first because he is the famous Saul Bellow and, secondly, because the black magic of print easily creates the impression of authority anyway – their personal right to judge as they judge will, as it were, change into a divine right – unless something is done about it. I have tried, and will try, to do something about it, first by writing the review and, secondly, by writing a full-length book about this single work,† and there won't be any destruction there, nor indeed much criticism.‡

In other words, my defensive anger about Bellow's narcissistic assumption that his impression was worth printing, or ethically printable (why worry about obscenity laws or, for that matter, the

---

★See Part I, pp. 56ff.
†(The author did indeed write this book, which will be published shortly. Ed.)
‡For a differentiation between criticism and analysis, which latter approach will be employed in my book on the Mendelssohn Concerto, see Part III, Section 2, pp. 134ff.

law of libel?) was the central source of my review. If the book had contained any first-hand information of substance, any first-hand thought other than semi-free associations, I should have said so. Since it contained nothing, I was determined to show that it contained nothing, and I do mean *show* – within the space at my disposal: the reader could judge for himself about the outer garment of God or about the importance of the information I provided about Justice Cohn's self-disqualification from the Eichmann trial. In short, my criticisms were either factual or else supported by evidence about which the reader could make up his own mind. What remained destructive, apart from the focal destruction of destruction, was the tone which, for better or worse, was deliberately discrediting: I considered that as Mendelssohn's professional counsel, I had something to be discrediting about.

The reason why I am making such a meal of explaining the principles behind this short book review is that they will be seen to be crucial to the argument I am attempting to evolve about critical destructiveness which, I am suggesting, is but one inevitable aspect, once a certain level of civilization has been reached, of that elemental, albeit exceptional intra-species destructiveness which sadly characterizes man.

A fact which has not, perhaps, received equal attention is that man is not only exceptional in killing members of his species; he is also exceptional in killing himself. In fact, the two tendencies go together, not just within the same species, but even, to a degree which has been statistically ascertained, within one and the same human being:*

> Carried to extremes, the paranoid attitude leads to murder; while the depressive attitude leads to suicide. That both mechanisms can be operative within the same individual (though not at exactly the same moment) is demonstrated by the fact that one in three murderers commit suicide. Indeed, D. J. West, in his study *Murder followed by Suicide* writes: 'Sometimes the aggressive urge is divided so evenly between homicidal and suicidal impulses that some quite trifling circumstance may have sufficient weight to tip the scales one way or the other.'†

> †The reference here is pp. 114ff; the year of publication is 1965 (both London and Cambridge, Mass.)

---

*A. Storr, op. cit., pp. 109–10.

This relation between homicide and suicide is borne out by various studies of the murder rates compared with the suicide rates in the Southern states of America. 'Austin Porterfield, in 1949, using mortality tables from *Vital Statistics*, brought the murder and suicide indices together and showed that there was a general inverse relationship between the two rates among the states . . .'*

*H. D. Graham and T. R. Gurr, *Violence in America*, New York, 1969.

I am not venturing the hope that upon reading this book, music critics will swerve over from their paranoid proclivities to wholesome depressions and commit suicide to any statistically rewarding extent; though my Preface held out the hope of some sunshine, we must not let the sun get the better of us to the point of unrealism. What I am venturing at this nodal intersection of our investigation needs a little introduction. Some diversion from the sordid business of destruction might, in any case, be welcome – but then again, we aren't moving all that far from it.

As a young man, at the invitation of the afore-mentioned J. C. Flugel,† I read a paper, under his chairmanship, to the British Psychological Society – at that time, I still *read* actual *papers* – on a subject on which (not knowing him personally) I had written him a long letter – a concept which I called 'Group Self-contempt'. I here wish to record, far too late, my gratitude to the professor, now dead, for his enthusiastic support of what I had to say: for an outsider, an unprofessional loner, it was quite an intellectual (and emotional) event which showed him that, although he would always want to be alone, he would never be lonely.

My simple submission was that wherever psycho-dynamically possible, (wo)man succeeded in having it both ways, or all ways, depending, of course, on the specific conflicting ways which the agencies at war with each other in the human mind wanted him or her to have it; and that group psychology, as distinct from individual psychology, offered rich opportunities of having things both ways, which was one reason why human beings, some of them, loved being members of groups.

Even of persecuted groups, and even if these persecuted groups were stable members of the society which persecuted them. In fact, this very situation presented an initial opportunity of having it both ways – of being a member of that society and of not being a

†See p. 89.

member. A deep-reaching further opportunity flowed from it.

Human beings loved despising others and, in their more depress-
ive moments, despising themselves. But it was not easy to despise
others and oneself at the same time if one was not a downright
psychopath: it wasn't easy to despise oneself when one felt big, or
others when one felt small. In the persecuted group, living within
the persecuting group, however, the phenomenon of 'group self-
contempt' could invariably be seen to emerge amongst a section of
its members as if by natural law – an attitude which made it
possible for the individual to extravert his moralistic aggression
inasmuch as he despised the other members of his group amongst
whom he felt himself to be an exception, and simultaneously to
introvert it inasmuch as he despised himself because he identified
himself with his group; the condition was that he projected his
superego on to the moral ideas of his society – which, after all, was
not an unusual thing to do. As examples of such group self-
contempt I listed Jewish anti-Semitism in the Diaspora,* with
which even an outstanding thinker like Otto Weininger† was affected, the prostitute's anti-prostitutionalism, of which I had made a
special study, and women's anti-feminism which, meanwhile, is
going almost as rapidly out of psychological fashion as Jewish
anti-Semitism has done in Israel, in proportion as the Women's Lib
movement is succeeding in its aims.

I did not, at the time, know about the correlation between, and
frequent interchangeability of, homicide and suicide, which was
discovered some ten years later. Had I known, I should not have
failed to point out that this factual evidence greatly strengthened
my theory – and that what the unique psychological bargain (in
terms of psychic economy) boiled down to was, symbolically, the
possibility of simultaneous homicide and suicide, to meet the
rarely-confessed, eminently human urge not to live and not to let
live – or to live and let live just a bit.

I am now in a position to make my suggestion based on the
valuable information we have gathered about human destructiveness in its extreme forms – on the basis, too, of my own

---

*In accordance with my theory, it has meanwhile vanished in Israel, where the
persecuting groups are surrounding the country, rather than being superimposed on
its society.
†See *Sex and Character*, London and New York, 1906.

destruction of Saul Bellow's criticism of Mendelssohn's Violin Concerto, or of the destruction (chiefly Cosima Wagner's) of western civilization's Wagner myth, or indeed of any of the countless destructions of destructive criticism which I have attempted throughout my writing life (I don't have a career and reject the concept, because a career turns you into a careerist). The psychology of group self-contempt gives us the clue. For a little group self-contempt wouldn't do the critic any harm. The trouble is that there isn't any articulate persecuting group on top – in an authoritative position, ready to have critical superegos projected on to it. The artists could be, if they had it in them from the point of view of what, in less sophisticated times, was known as guts. They have the authority within the world of the mind – at least those do who are, rightly or wrongly, considered leading artists by their contemporary society. And they certainly have, all but the worst, a potentially persecuting attitude towards the critics; not to put too fine a point on it, they loathe them. As a teacher, coach, and adviser of artists, I have, perhaps, a wider and deeper experience of their all too private feelings about the critical profession than anybody else, and I give it as my well-tested opinion that at least within the musical world, there isn't a single artist of substance whose attitude towards the critical profession is not more or less unqualifiedly hostile – a *fact* which is never as much as mentioned, let alone discussed in its horrifying implications. The reason is that the artist, especially the artist of substance, tends to put all his considerable guts into his art, and all his often considerable cowardice, opportunism, and defensive seclusion into his life: he doesn't want to be bothered, and can you blame him. What a terrible thought it would be if a Benjamin Britten had wanted to be bothered. I am taking him as an example because I know, first-hand, that he accepted my own views on criticism without reservation – despite the considerable success he enjoyed amongst critics in his lifetime, rather exceptionally so amongst musical geniuses.

On second thoughts, however, the fact that the critics do not have an authoritative, persecuting group above them may not be regrettable; it may be, from the standpoint of a possible realistic development of group self-contempt, a blessing. Realistically, that is to say, nothing can be advanced in favour of the group self-contempt of a Jew, a woman, even a prostitute. It follows that morally, the attitude will always affect the weakest, the most gutless members of the group – for even an Otto Weininger, intellectually a man of genius, was morally weak. In this pseudo-scientific age, in which moral values (as distinct from hidden, creeping moralizations) are not discussed by 'rational' (rationalizing) people because they cannot count upon universal agreement, it simply is not done to talk about moral weakness in a book with some scientific pretensions – but that's the age's problem, not mine. Mine is indeed the immorality of criticism as it stands, which evinces a triple aspect – the harm it does to art, the harm it does to the artist and, above all, its unchallengeability from within the profession, unless you are prepared to be an unprofessional professional. Now, if it were decided from within – say, to begin with, at a meeting of the Critics' Circle, which spends its time talking about nothing – to abandon the firm convention of mutual peaceability and, on the contrary, open the door to, and encourage the criticism of criticism, this *realistic* opportunity to have it both ways without superimposed authority, without any projection of conscience on to a critic-despising, parental body, would only be seized by the morally strongest, by thinking individuals rather than feeling sub-groups. It would be they who would see that those who sit in judgement must be challengeable, otherwise there cannot be any justice – and if criticism does not admit that it presumes to dispense justice, how does it explain and defend the very act of criticizing, which is an act of judging?

Rational group self-contempt, simultaneous aesthetic homicide and suicide, would be the next best thing to undermining the phoney, but none the less effective authority of criticism altogether – a sociological impossibility. The critic's unusually strong destructive urges, without which he wouldn't have become a critic, would find a new and potentially constructive outlet – the paradigm, in fact, of constructive destructiveness, which is defensive attack. And the fact that the impulses behind it would be individually moral rather than collectively moralistic would ensure a high level of competence, for incompetence is, ultimately, a moral weakness, i.e. concealment, or else ignorance, of ignorance.

That only the morally strong, the self-aware anti-phoneys, would choose to have it both ways, to be critics and anti-critics at the same time, is even superficially evident as soon as we think in practical terms: the calling would still be an uphill job, without much prospect of material reward. No newspaper or journal would want an anti-critical column, or would want its critical columns messed up by intermittent anti-criticism. Critics are often loud in their complaints about the uncivilized, inartistic demands of their editors, but fundamentally, the two phoney professions play into each other's dirty hands: for both of them, art is material, not the end, and neither of them has ever dreamt of the simple, reality-saving possibility of making criticism the material instead, towards the end of art.

Again, amongst his brethren, the group-contemptuous critic would remain as unpopular as the anti-Semitic Jew is amongst Jews, the anti-prostitutional prostitute amongst prostitutes, and the feminine derogator of women amongst women. The fact that they are wrong and he would be right would intensify rather than reduce his unpopularity. Though there would be brothers-in-arms, he would still remain alone, because any joint intellectual action would undermine the very foundation of his calling, which would be the unhindered exercise of individual judgement on judgement: untruths, like truths, are not discovered in committee.

I was not, it must be realized, even born the day before yesterday. The naïvety of my utopia is not studied, but it is conscious nevertheless. However, the temptation of conjuring up, for once, a realistic utopia cannot be resisted, and the fact that it is unlikely to be realized does not make it any less realistic. Nor am I all that sure that it will remain without a trace of realization: naïvely or not, I am confident that in their entirety, our deductions – strictly, logically speaking, they are really empirical inductions – will make one or the other critic, in whichever art, think again. Such reconsideration will not only be due to whatever logical power my argument may possess, but also to its appeal to the basic requirements of human conscience – not to harm people, and to resist the harming of people.

When I said that nobody ever dreamt of the simple reality-saving possibility of turning criticism, instead of art, into material, I was not, in the first place, complaining about human stupidity – or if I was, I meant by stupidity something as which it is not generally taken, to wit, very often, *a function of cowardice*. The degree to which people cannot understand is, more often than not, as nothing to the degree to which they do not want to understand. In this age in which, for the time being, heroism is a thing of the past, it is not easy to recommend understanding by drawing attention to the fact that in many critical situations, understanding is an act of heroism, but the fact remains, and there is always the consoling consideration that heroism may well be a thing of the future too. It is certainly an act of unobtrusive, individual heroism that is required for the simple understanding of the harmfulness, the unmitigated destructiveness of most criticism of the arts. Every artist agrees: what right has every critic to disagree? Or, if he doesn't disagree, what right has he not to do something about this totally neglected side of humanity's greatest problem – man's need to destroy?

In any case, we have now cleared the air so far as the general problem of criticism is concerned, to the extent of letting the sun shine on those who might choose to sit in a sunny place. From such a vantage point, they could help, not only to make an honest profession out of the phoney profession of criticism, but to tackle the problem of the other phoney professions too: inasmuch as the elemental critical element in them was discredited, they, likewise, would have to think again about themselves, and channel their destructive energies in this new direction.

The general problem of criticism is one thing, music criticism not quite another, but an overlapping one: some of its questions it shares with all other brands of criticism, some important others are unique to the criticism of the only art that – to put it as crudely as possible, but quite precisely at the same time – isn't based on pictures, is wholly independent of the sense of sight; perhaps this is why, as even many painters (including Francis Bacon★) agree, its sense of insight may be altogether strongest among the arts. All the others, in any case, either depend on visual images or on conceptual thought, and verbal concepts are, in the last resort, derived from visual impressions too. As we turn our attention to music criticism alone, however, we shall not confine ourselves to its lonely problems, but shall take in some which it shares with the criticism of visual art; the only reason why I shall not concern myself with the latter is that I am not competent to do so.

★Private communication.

Part III

MUSIC CRITICISM

1 Critical Torture

'There is no short answer to the problem of human destructiveness,' says Anthony Storr in conclusion of his fascinating and comprehensive study. 'Let us hope that a longer look at the way the human animal develops may eventually produce some modification in our violent and destructive species.'* It is doubtful, though, whether man is, meanwhile, entitled yet to call himself an animal, and the longer look will have to concern itself, in particular, with an aspect of violence and destructiveness which is quite specifically human, and that is torture. Nor does torture always own up to its motives or its nature; on the contrary, it easily appears in the clothes of a comforting or at least helpful activity, even of healing: two examples have already been given in this book, i.e. the electrical treatment of war neurotics in the First World War, and electro-convulsive therapy before it was applied under a general anaesthetic.†

The critic, too, poses as a helper, sometimes even a healer, or at least a teacher, but the pose does not acquit him of torture where torture occurs; in fact, one or the other reader may be inclined to agree that we have reached a stage in our examination of the critic's role which justifies our considering the critic guilty unless he can be proved innocent. Nevertheless, so far as the specific charge of torture is concerned, we shall now proceed to prove the music critic guilty in two ways – one very particular, and one very general.

The particular way is quickly outlined. Just because there is all the difference in the mental world between musical thought and conceptual thought, the music critic finds it relatively easy not to

---

*op. cit., p. 115.
†See pp. 69 and 81.

let his reader know what he is talking about – and if his reader is the
artist, and his aim condemnation, the artist is submitted to torture.
I know the situation from the receiving end, for many have been
the occasions when I have received press cuttings, of notices or
reviews, from artists I have taught or coached, plaintively or
aggressively asking me, according to temperament, the rhetorical
question what the critic was on about, and whether I, being myself
practised as a critic, could make any sense of his unfavourable
opinion at all. The artist is thus frequently placed in the precise
position of K., the anti-hero in Kafka's *Trial*, who is pronounced
guilty of he knows not what, and is duly executed in the end – as
indeed the artist is. As an extreme example, it will be useful to
remember here the erstwhile *Times* critic's verdict that Schoenberg
was not a composer at all:* we were never allowed to fathom why
exactly Schoenberg was no composer, though the article in question was of considerable length. At the same time, there is a
decisive difference between the tortured K. and the tortured artist.
Seen from the point of view of God, K. *is* guilty – of being no more
than a moral mediocrity, average man for once personified – like
Gregor Samsa in 'Metamorphosis'. Whereas the artist may be
innocent when seen from the point of view of God – except that the
critic is God, being the only omniscient and unchallengeable
authority that has been revealed to us, even though he may not be
able to read a score or know the difference between Haydn's key of
F minor, Mozart's key of G minor, Beethoven's of C minor,
Mendelssohn's of E minor, Schoenberg's of D minor and a
latchkey.

What makes such torture particularly painful is that often, the
fata morgana of meaning arises before the victim's eyes, like the
mirage of an oasis which the man dying of thirst in the desert sees
emerge before him: as he painfully moves nearer, the oasis escapes.
The instrument of torture which the critic here employs, without
the remotest attempt at substantiation (which, in any case, he
would find impossible), are words which we use in order to describe conceptual, verbal sense-making and nonsense-making:
'argument', 'consistency', 'validity', 'logic', 'well-reasoned' or
'badly reasoned', 'fallacy', 'contradiction' are favourite metaphors
of high criticism of musical composition. There certainly is such a

---

*See my Preface, p. 4.

thing as musical logic, but since no critic using the concept of logic has ever disclosed what it is, it must remain meaningless to the most knowledgeable addressee, all the more so since the concept of contradiction, which is often employed in the same devastating breath, is not applicable, as unfavourable criticism, to musical logic at all.

The teacher of composition, as distinct from the critic, really has to worry about the justifiability of these instruments of torture; even though he may be a would-be torturer (as so many phoney professionals are), they won't be of much avail to him in private, where he can be challenged. In my own, unwritten 'paper' at the previously-mentioned symposium on music criticism at McMaster University in Canada,* I tried this very thing – to define the laws of musical thought, in the context of my theory of music which underlies functional analysis – my wordless method of musical analysis.† The difference between verbal thought and musical thought, I suggested, was demonstrably diametrical. Verbal, conceptual thought was essentially static, whereas musical thought was essentially dynamic. If this differentiation was true, it followed that the laws of musical thought must be the exact opposite of the laws of conceptual thought – which, in fact, they could be shown to be.

The laws of logical (conceptual) thought are really axioms, in the sense that they are incapable of proof (as distinct from exemplification) and are not, in fact, by the very nature of human reasoning, considered to stand in need of proof. *Mutatis mutandis*, precisely the same could be said of musical thought, of musical logic, which are just as binding. Only, the intellect to which you submit the validly axiomatic nature of the laws of musical logic has to be as intelligent musically as the intellect of the consenting recipient of the validly axiomatic nature of the laws of conceptual thought has to be intelligent verbally.

The axioms of conceptual reasoning are in fact three; whether they need be three is another question – for they do seem to me to bear slightly obsessional traits, inasmuch as they say the same thing three times over. But let us not enter into a superfluous quarrel with the logicians, professionally obsessional as they have to be: the thing itself is right, in however many ways you say it, and the

---

*See pp. 33–4.
†About which a little more in Section 2, p. 134 below.

different ways may be said to illuminate different aspects of the same proposition, or satisfy different types of intellectual receptivity.

Axiom No. 1, then, is the famous Law of Identity, which says that everything is what it is – or, in symbolical form, that A=A. Axiom No. 2 is the Law of Contradiction, of particular interest to us since we are often puzzled by critical reproaches to the effect that a composer is contradicting himself. It says that a thing cannot both be something and not be something – or, in symbolical form, that A=B precludes the possibility of A=non-B. Axiom No. 3 is known as the Law of Excluded Middle, and says that a thing either is something or it is not something – or, in symbolical form, that A either is or is not B.

Meaningful musical thought develops on the basis of a precise inversion of these axioms: a motif or phrase or period can only acquire and accumulate meaning in the course of a composition if it does not remain what it is; in order to evince musical logic it must develop into something else and yet remain itself, so that it turns out to be both something and not something. In our last section,* I shall explain how precisely musical logic (if any!) operates and can therefore be shown not to operate when it doesn't; in the present context of critical torture it is enough to point out that unless there is recognition of the laws of musical thought and the way in which some terms of conceptual logic (e.g. 'validity') can be made to apply to musical logic and some others (e.g. 'contradiction') can't – unless, in short, their relevance is proved by illustration, their use is the purest torture; for is there worse intellectual torture imaginable than wholly irrelevant criticism that gives itself the successful appearance of total relevance? As we shall see presently, there is a type of critical torture which is yet worse, but it is not intellectual. Meanwhile, we note that it is in this torturing situation that the music critic (like many another phoney professional, from the witch-pricker onwards) gives the most unblemished demonstration of his phoniness, of his creation of unsolvable problems.

The absolute requirement for evidence, illustration, exemplification would powerfully reduce the victim's risk of not knowing what the critic is talking about – or everybody else's bafflement, for that matter, except for those who happen to share the critic's

---

*See pp. 155ff.

prejudices, and to whom, victim apart, his criticisms are addressed: as it stands, music criticism is a family affair. In literary criticism, exemplification is more frequent in proportion as it is easier, and it is easier because in that intellectual area, verbal criticism deals with a verbal art or craft. My review of Saul Bellow's book about Israel is, partly, a piece of literary criticism,* and when I accuse him of repetitiveness, or of writing kitsch, or of omitting essential information, or indeed of factual errors, I give examples of each: it is up to the reader whether he calls kitsch what I call kitsch, whether my information is essential, and so forth. The question of guilty or not guilty is thus ideally made a matter for the jury: in the capacity not only of counsel for the prosecution and/or defence, but also of a judge in this downright legalistic sense, an expert who investigates the case and sums it up, the critic renounces torture altogether and, in fact, leaves all phoney activity behind him.

The fact remains that in music criticism, too, both of composition and of performance, the adduction of evidence is, within limits, possible, and that the limits are definable. I am thinking of essential limits, not of the incidental complications created by, say, the requirements of newspapers, the limited space they are willing to grant to their music critic, or their unwillingness to print music-type examples, except occasionally as an incomprehensible ornament. There are two dimensions to musical meaning: there is what I call 'local' meaning – say, the meaning of a tune or even a phrase, regardless of its structural context – and there is 'total' meaning, which is the meaning of this entity as an element of the entire structure, regardless of its local beauty. On the highest level of meaningfulness, however, regardlessness is transmuted into regardfulness: local meaning does not forget total meaning, and total meaning does not allow any local element to be boring in itself. But even when they are thus ideally co-ordinated – and indeed demonstrable along a system of two co-ordinates – local and total meaning are still separately assessable.

Now, local meaning, or lack of local meaning, can be exemplified, whereas total meaning can't (except by my wordless functional analysis): these are the simple limits of critical evidence, but they still leave considerable room for the collection and demonstration of evidence which can be submitted in music type, and

*See p. 56.

verbally integrated into the judge's summing up – no torture left, at least on our present count, for however wrong one may be, the composer or player knows what one is talking about, and irrelevance thus exposes itself.

In what I now regard as my critical student years, I experimented a great deal with this type of evidencing, not only in my writings on composition, but also in my reviews of performances: essential characteristics of interpretation are easily notatable; in fact, in the late nineteenth and early twentieth century, they *were* notated in advance by a number of composers themselves – often to a fault, inhibiting the performer, as some of them later came to realize: Reger, Bartók and Schoenberg are outstanding examples. The late twentieth-century tendency to leave everything to the performer can, in fact, partly be seen as a reaction against the early twentieth-century tendency to leave nothing to him – and, like all mere reactions, it has proved rather fruitless and may be on the way out by the time the present book is in print.

Logically fond as I am of extreme examples, I am trying to recall one or two of the very few occasions when, having – as I rightly or wrongly thought – attained critical mastery, I criticized local meaning in the great masterpieces of the great masters, submitting my evidence and leaving the final decision, I hope, to the jury. One prominent double example was my criticism of the themes of the opening movement and the minuet of Mozart's famous 'Hunt' Quartet, K. 458 – the first of his two great B flat quartets, which may indeed have attained its disproportionate popularity (disproportionate, that is, when compared with the frequency with which his other master quartets and quintets are played and listened to) – because of the relative primitiveness of these two tunes, rather than as a result of its sublime slow movement: I have never yet seen a sublime slow movement make a work popular.

However that may be, there seems little doubt that on this occasion, Mozart was stung, by an unknown motive, into trying his hand at folkloristic melodic invention – to which he could feel rather partial anyway, as his later inventions for Papageno in *The Magic Flute* showed. In any case, within the German-singing world, the folk-song means something entirely different from what it means to an Englishman, a Scotsman or, for that matter, a Hungarian, Czech, or an inhabitant of any of the Balkan countries: without a single exception, all German folk-songs are rubbish, and whenever great composers used them (which wasn't all that often anyway), they used them without compositorial respect, but purely as material whose value simply lay in the associations it aroused: Schoenberg's use (and destruction) of 'O du lieber Augustin' in his Second Quartet is an illuminating example. To adopt a folkloristic style without sinking into banality was, therefore, difficult, and my prosecution plea is that in 'The Hunt', Mozart, demonstrably, did not succeed.

With a music example, the evidence can be submitted almost wordlessly, merely by marking the operative, I mean the inoperative spots in the two tunes, but it isn't all that difficult either to say what the music example would show – a reminder, this, that the practical impossibility of printing music type is not always an acceptable excuse. All that is required is for the reader to look up the score himself if he doesn't remember the melodies anyway.

Both the theme of the first movement and that of the minuet fail to generate forward-urging tension because they return to the tonic too often and too soon. In the case of the opening movement's first subject, moreover, repetitiveness is intensified by three of the five occurrences of the tonic being part of the identical cadential motif, while the fourth and fifth, at two notes' distance, are part of the sister motif which concludes the perfect cadence of the square, eight-bar sentence. For in no other mature sonata movement did Mozart conceive a subject of similar simple-mindedness, and Papageno's 'Der Vogelfänger bin ich ja' (which bears structural resemblances) is a sublime shape in comparison.

Again, in the theme of the minuet, Mozart returns to the tonic three times at the respective beginnings of the last three bars of the eight-bar melody that forms the first part of the theme; with its repeat, we thus get six occurrences, all melodically descending from the supertonic, which once more means, despite some harmonic enlivening, repeated relaxation of tension before there is enough tension to relax – a debit account of relaxation, as it were, which can only be paid back by the total structure (with interest, to be sure), not locally. However strong Mozart's folkloristic intentions, under the influence, perhaps, of all the rotten tunes he was thinking of, he here, in both these themes, went far beyond anything he himself regarded as aesthetically permissible on any other occasion. For the rest, I have gone into much greater detail here than in the past – reprimanding myself retrospectively, maybe, that

I myself may not have made absolutely sure that everybody knew what I was talking about.

Another example of defective great mastery, objectively demonstrable, is the opening of the last movement of Dvořák's far too little played Violin Concerto: we can ill afford to neglect one of the none too many great *and* violinistic works in this curious genre, where greatness almost invariably goes together with problems, or at least unease, from the point of view of the solo instrument, at any rate from the outset of the history of the grand concerto: Beethoven, Schumann, Brahms, Tchaikovsky, Schoenberg, Bartók and Stravinsky are prominent examples. However, the theme of the Dvořák finale does not immediately get across what it is intended to get across – what is indeed an essential element of its rhythmic layout: the tension between its ⅜ metre, the rhythmic background as I call it, and the rhythmic foreground, which is un-notated, but heard ¾. It is, in fact, only ¾ that one hears to begin with; the implication of the actual, notated metre, against the background of which the theme forms its syncopations, do not emerge until the ninth bar, which discloses the three-quaver beat for the first time: until then, the all-important syncopations simply are not heard unless you know the work or have the score in front of you. If you don't and haven't, you are traumatically compelled to rehear the first eight bars retrospectively in view of what you now realize is their metre. All that Dvořák would have had to do would have been to insert the selfsame quaver upbeat with which he introduces the consequent in bar ten at the beginning of the antecedent, i.e. the very beginning – an upbeat which, no doubt, he suppressed in order to make the structure yet more interesting, compact, unconventional, unexpected. So influenced was he by his own awareness of the metre, which was staring him in the face, that he didn't realize what he had done – that now the listener would not immediately be aware of it, and hence would miss the basic rhythmic tension, not hearing inside him the strong beats of the bar which are silenced by the syncopations. As a positive example for comparison – of a drastic tension between metre and rhythm which is so consistent and continuous that the rhythm amounts to a polymetric texture, we might take the minuet from Haydn's D major String Quartet, Op. 20, No.4, where the notated minuet metre is clearly contradicted, throughout the principal section, by a 'merely' heard gavotte rhythm – ¾ by 4/4, with the simultaneous patterns being audible from the moment go and indeed all the way.

Now, were Mozart and Dvořák alive, I am certain that they would (A) have known what I was talking about, and so not have suspected me of attempted torture, and (B) have agreed, in fact, with my criticisms, and done something about them – all the more readily so since I would not have made them in public: in their lifetimes, they would have been my only possible addressees, since my plea would not have been a matter for the jury at all, as I would have been pleading negligence towards their own intentions rather than towards anybody else. My criticisms would, in fact, have stood or fallen with the composers' agreement.

I have adumbrated the problem of private versus public criticism both in my Preface and in my autobiographical observations on the conducting of a master class,* and it is indeed the public exposure of what should, perhaps, be private criticism which brings me to my second way, the very general one, in which I consider the music critic guilty of torture unless he proves himself innocent.

Man has a passion for talking to the wrong people when he finds something wrong with his fellow men: he will but rarely complain *to* the person he is complaining *about*; in fact, language itself, with its crucial 'about' and its refusal to make a complaint straight-forwardly transitive, confirms our reluctance to address it to its proper addressee. If I am entitled to complain *about* you, why should I not be able to complain *you*? To my knowledge, no language makes provision for what would at once be the most logical and the most ethical course of action: thus stupidity makes cowards of us all and, earlier in the vicious circle, cowardice idiots. My little statistical sample of the proportion of criticism in people's conversations† could never have been supplied if most of that criticism had not been made *in absentia*; in fact, veritable revolutions would be afoot if people started addressing their criticisms to their objects. Tact, (black) discretion, practicability, sheer personal safety and security are advanced as reasons for such chronic dis-placement of criticism whenever the displacer is challenged; but together with his partners in conversation, he will hasten to make clear that, by the very nature of his challenge, the challenger must be

---

*See pp.5 and 78 respectively.
†See p. 90.

considered a bit of an odd fellow, insensitive to the niceties and refinements of personal and professional intercourse.

Yet, when we enter any of the professionally local pubs of an evening after office hours, and even if we are complete strangers to the people at whose table we happen to sit down, we shall soon be regaled – admittedly under the influence of alcohol which frees, not courage, but unthinking and unconstructive, misplaced daring – with moralistic, self-righteous stories about the misdeeds and general objectionability of bosses, colleagues, or about the irrational structure of the business or organization or institution in which the speaker is working: he may be discreet and tactful in the conversations with his bosses and colleagues, but he certainly is not discreet and tactful in this conversation with us. And, sure enough, if, in such a moment, highly charged with emotion however jocular in well practised conversational form, we simply ask, 'Why do you tell me? Why don't you tell them?' we do, upon occasion, produce a highly-charged silence too, an impression that the message has gone home, or visited home for a while anyway; for most minds prefer to spend their time abroad, for entirely plausible reasons: at home, the human mind tends to be more heavily taxed. In any event, rendered a little reckless ourselves by a drug which is a psychological status symbol where, say, cannabis is a sign of delinquency, we leave the pub wondering whether man ever talks to other men, or whether he just needs other men in order to talk to himself. I once had a secretary who, at moments of outwardly-induced stress, and if she thought herself unobserved, audibly complained to herself about the (easily demonstrable) inadequacies of the powers that be – and who, when she was thus observed by her colleagues, was deemed a bit weird. But the very same colleagues used each other as more or less willing material, usually less, for their unconfessed monologues – so just as alcohol can be argued to be more harmful than cannabis, my ex-secretary's colleagues could be argued to be far weirder than she was – if, indeed, we are entitled to consider her weird at all.

Our present concern is a kind of human weirdness so universal that it has no chance, or faces no risk, of being recognized for what it is. At the same time, if there is one thing that is worse, again both logically and ethically, than complaining about other people in their absence, it is complaining about them in their presence – not *to* them, however, but to other people, without their being able to defend themselves. In courts of law all over the civilized world, severe precautions are taken for the listening object of criticism, the defendant in a criminal case, to have the opportunity, if not indeed the duty, to answer back; but the object, or the author of the object, of unfavourable music criticism is *a priori* condemned to listen in silence to what ought to have been addressed to him, rather than to others, in the first place. His silence is likely to be all the more pronounced since, even if he were sufficiently heedless of elementary convention to wish to break it, and even if he knew what the critic was talking about, he would most probably find it difficult to verbalize his musical reflections – an act, not of translation (which is impossible, because music, as opposed to language, is not a language*) but of remote self-reportage which needs a lifetime of practice and presupposes a spontaneous interest in verbal thought such as only a few musicians possess.

Assuming that our first-discussed instrument of torture has not been used, and that it is therefore tolerably clear what the unfavourable critic is talking about, he is, according to the afore-mentioned Law of Excluded Middle, either right or not right – and, though he would often have it otherwise when driven into a corner, he cannot, according to the Law of Contradiction, both be and not be right: if this is the way his logic works, he had better abandon conceptual thought and become a composer – although, from our point of view, his abandoning conceptual thought would be quite good enough.

If, then, he is not right, the publication of his opinion is, ethically, libel – and by ethical libel I mean something closely definable: the moral reasons responsible for the various laws of libel in different legal systems can be shown to obtain in the case of unjustified, damaging, unfavourable criticism of music or musical performance. All such criticism would be unjustified if, legally speaking, a plea of justification could not be successful; and a plea of justification could not, or should not, be successful if the critic is not right. It has to be admitted, at the same time, that torture cannot reasonably be shown to have been practised if the critic is wrong, even though he may have intended to torture.

Where torture comes in with a vengeance for misdeeds not committed – unless a simple failure of communication be judged to

---

*See p. 47.

be such a misdeed – is where the critic is right. He tells, and doesn't tell, the composer or performer where he went wrong: he addresses the public and so degrades the proper addressee of his complaint to the role of a silently suffering eavesdropper – even though, to try to save his soul, he may cheat himself into believing that he addresses the composer or performer and allows the public to eavesdrop to the extent of paying for his living – for the artist would certainly never do so. Or maybe the public wouldn't either if newspaper editors hadn't decided that it would, though it has to be admitted that there is little torture hiding behind authoritative benefaction which does not easily find public support, for torture by proxy, passive connivance, saves one much of the unease one might feel if one undertook the torture oneself.

In any case, the critic's official addressee is the wrong addressee, and if he pretends to himself that he is 'really' addressing the artist he poses as the artist's teacher; in fact, if his criticism is to the point, for its duration, he *is* the artist's teacher and finds himself in the situation of a teacher in a master class, only worse: in the artist's cognitive presence, but his physical absence, he uses him, his temporary student, as material for his lecture to the public. In short, with perfect ease, he has changed over from one phoney profession to another – or rather, he is pursuing both of them, in that he helps in the creation and combination of either's problems, and helps to leave them unsolved.

I put it to the reader and, in particular, the music critic that only if one has been both a critic and a teacher, and only if one has criticized and taught in the same areas – composition, performance – is one in a position to gauge the extent to which one's addressing oneself to the wrong people, with the right person's knowledge, represents an act of mental torture if what one says is right: on the basis of what is, in ethical principle, an act of betrayal – for all weaknesses are secrets before their rightful owner chooses to disclose them – one adds incurable injury to unanswerable insult, degradation to public exposure. These are dramatic words, but the critic-cum-teacher knows, has learnt by painful experience, that they do not dramatize; they merely factually report. An insult is a psychological fact, that is, if the person alleged to have been insulted feels insulted, nor is it the degrader whom we are inviting to decide upon the facts of degradation.

As simultaneous critic and teacher, watchful of the effect on

one's activities, one unwittingly produces a controlled experiment
– if, that is to say, one has anything of relevance to communicate;
and if one hasn't, one is unlikely to remain a teacher for long, at any
rate on a level which makes the effects of one's public criticisms and
one's teaching comparable. But when one teaches the kind of artist
one criticizes and is, maybe, lucky or unlucky enough successively
to extend one's critical and one's educational insights to the same
distinguished victim, one comes to realize that one and the same
relevant criticism is likely to have the opposite effect according to
whether it is made in public, to the wrong addressee, as a complaint
about the artist as it were, or in private, as a function of a relationship in which weaknesses are easily disclosed without any ensuing
feeling of degradation, because the joint endeavour is to turn them
into strengths – and if the artist is sufficiently gifted, there is little to
compare to the strength of a weakness overcome or transmuted.

In response to artistically justified, public criticism, the artist will
put up all the psychological defences at his disposal and will firmly
deny to himself the relevance of anything unfavourable that has
been said about his work: the critic will have succeeded in his most
ignoble task, the creation of a profound and insoluble psychological
and aesthetic problem. Insoluble, that is, unless he turns himself
into a teacher without submitting to the phoniness of that profession in its turn, and goes about the business of repairing the damage
he has done. He will then notice that in private, if he identifies
himself with the artist rather than demanding that the artist should
identify with his ideas about our art, the type of criticism, perhaps
even the very same criticism, he used to make in public, far from
being defensively rejected, will be turned into self-criticism in no
time, and unless he cannot stem his desire to hold forth, he will be
able to say good-night before the lesson is, or the lessons are over –
before, I mean, a transference situation develops which makes the
artist dependent on the teacher, depersonalizes him, and reinstates
the teacher's professional phoniness; otherwise, if he isn't careful,
before the teacher knows where he is, the artist will turn him into a
'great teacher' in no time, which is a fate worse than death – worse,
that is, than being a despicable critic. For the rest, the difference
between the artist's reaction against a piece of public criticism and
his reaction to the same meaningful criticism made to him directly
in private is a measure of the degree of torture the public criticism
amounts to.

At the start of this section, I promised to prove the music critic guilty of torture in two ways – or should I now say, most critics? Let us not be rash. In any case, I withheld a third way because, at that stage, I wanted the reader and myself to agree, at least, on the concept of torture as such. But by way of a violently extended, developmental coda of downright Beethovenian proportions, I should now like to introduce the concept of posthumous torture and thus bring another charge of torture against the critic which the jury might not even be prepared to consider, since it does some violence to the meaning of torture. But let me at least be heard; if the jury then decides to advise the judge that there is no case to answer, so be it.

The ground has been prepared by our associating torture with libel, or rather with an insulting and damaging and degrading action which is all the more hurtful in all these respects for not being capable of being legally described as libel: the only reason why it's not libel is that it's worse. Now, independently of the problem of criticism of the arts, though nowise outside the problem of criticism as such, it has always struck me as unreasonable as well as indecent that as soon as somebody is dead, the law allows us to talk or write about him in a way which, were he alive, would be actionable. Why should his reputation be safeguarded when he is alive, but not when he is dead? Those, especially, who are talked and written about after their death are likely to have lived, to some extent at least, for posterity, and quite possibly, they are more interested in keeping their posthumous reputation intact than in leading an uninsulted life. In addition, there are the feelings of those to consider who identify with the dead person either because of the value of his personality and work or because they were close to him anyway – as relatives, lovers, friends. A striking example from modern times was the film, *Death in Venice*, in which Mahler was turned into a homosexual. I am not suggesting that homosexuality is something bad or abnormal; what I am saying is that in a society dominated by heterosexuals, the homosexual will easily be regarded as something bad or abnormal (with the result, incidentally, that some homosexuals evince the attitude of group self-contempt described in Part II above★). It follows that few who are not homosexuals will regret the fact, or will not object to being

---

★See pp. 105ff.

thought of or described as homosexuals – just as few men will not mind being considered feminine, and few Gentiles will not mind being regarded as Jews. In a celebrated, protracted civil action in pre-Hitler Austria, where anti-Semitism was a crime, a man was convicted of slander because he had called another a Jew, and although he had pleaded justification: the other was, in fact, a Jew. The judge ruled that while being a Jew was not something bad, the defendant's calling the plaintiff a Jew sprang from the intention of calling him something bad.

A heterosexual, then, may justly regard his being described as a pansy or queer or queen as an insult, however noble the history of homosexuality from Socrates to Benjamin Britten, and there is no doubt that Mahler, had he been alive, would yet more easily have succeeded in an action against the film-maker than did that Viennese Jew against his offender, for while the Jew was a Jew, Mahler was not a homosexual. But had he been alive, the film could not, of course, have been made, while as a dead man, he is without protection. One gathers that his sculptor-daughter was deeply distressed about the film and wanted to bring an action – but could not, of course, do so. In the circumstances, I consider it is fair to say that posthumous libel subjected her to torture quite apart from the posthumous torture to which Mahler himself may be said to have been subjected – a torture which, live, affects all others who have, not for the flimsiest of reasons, identified with the genius. Do we appreciate the irony of the legal situation? Our Jew was sufficiently protected against insult to win a case against somebody who spoke the truth, whereas the dead Mahler is so unprotected against insult that his daughter can't bring a case against a lie.

De mortuis nil nisi bene* has always struck me as irrational, too – just as irrational as its inversion, regularly practised by music critics in particular. We writers on music (and film makers about music, Ken Russell being the prime example) seem to be incapable of adopting a rational, realistic attitude towards the dead. When a great composer is safely buried, that is, we stand the Latin proverb on its head, have a go at him and take it out of him – out of the man, anyway: overdue revenge for his music which, unpictorial and unverbal, presumes yet further above man's station, more mystically and more awe-inspiringly so, than do the other arts. The

---

*'Speak only good of the dead.'

entire Wagner myth,* posthumous torture achieved by historical
'objectivity', could not have developed if the composer had been
protected by the law of libel as if he had been alive; the truth, the
sheer facts of the case of Wagner, would not have had to go
underground for close on a century. A corpse cannot sue of course,
nor would the possibility of an action have to be made dependent
on his next of kin moving into litigation: the state would be the
protector of the dead and bring prosecutions against libel or slander
of the dead. It would thus become even more dangerous to malign
those who can no longer fight for themselves than to libel the
living, for those who damage the reputation of the dead would be
guilty of criminal slander or criminal libel. Nor again would there
be any risk of a cover-up, of the law helping towards hiding the
truth – for if a state proceeded against an individual who, say, had
written a book about the criminality of Adolf Hitler, the defendant
could successfully plead justification and, in such a blatant case,
demand costs from the state, all of which would, of course, prevent
the state from prosecuting in the first place.

In the course of my writing this book, Benjamin Britten has died
and posthumous libel, posthumous critical torture, has moved into
action without a moment's hesitation – but only in England: it is
fascinating to observe that, for instance, the Germans, less under
the immediate threat of his awe-ful, truthful music than we, were
far more generous about it ('one of the greatest composers', 'a great
genius'), and left the man alone altogether, whereas Martin
Cooper, in the *Daily Telegraph* of 6 December 1976 (Britten having
died on 4 December) found it necessary to review 'the man and his
music', and to torture him a little posthumously in the process.
Historical objectivity could at long last have its say, the body
having been moved out of the way. I hope I may count Martin
Cooper† amongst my friends; if so, friend will here eat friend – a
disloyal practice which, I need hardly stress at this late stage in our
cogitations, I deem, upon occasion, an absolute ethical necessity
within the world of criticism.

To begin with, Mr Cooper gave expression to the music critic's
ill-disguised dream – the dead composer, whose death was more
timely than you and I, being preoccupied with the development of

---

*See pp. 95ff.
†d. 1986.

his music, may have thought in our uncritical innocence: 'Benjamin Britten's . . . creative career has spanned the middle third of the century and has only been cut short by a death that is to our way of thinking untimely, though few of the great composers of the past have lived longer.' That makes their deaths untimely, too (as one has always felt in the case of, say, a Beethoven or Mahler), not his timely. But worse was to come:

> . . . he remained shy and intensely sensitive, ill at ease on public occasions and fully himself only among his close friends, of whom he demanded nothing less than a lifetime of unblemished loyalty.
> This note of emotional immaturity in the man had its happy reflection in the artist's understanding of children and in the childlike, unspoiled capacity for wonder, for infusing new life and individuality into a familiar situation, a well-worn harmony or melodic phrase, that is a characteristic of all his best music.

Historical objectivity works wonders, miracles: no sooner has one dutifully discovered that there is something rotten in the state of greatness, than the rottenness has 'happy reflections' in the greatness – and can one be more fair-minded, despite having prac-tised critical torture on the way? The trouble is that in the circum-stances, all this negative evaluation doesn't mean a thing.

In fact, it doesn't mean anything without the circumstances either; it is a pure reflection of the critic's own emotional diffi-culties. I shouldn't be so rash as to talk about 'emotional immatur-ity' – a phoney critical concept if ever there was one, unsupportable by any but the most primitive amateur psychiatry. What Martin Cooper is no doubt referring to, or justifying his remote diagnosis with, is Britten's homosexuality. Amongst schematic psychiatrists, admittedly, homosexuality is held to be a sign of immaturity – especially in England, where the educational system tends to pro-duce a homosexual stage in adolescence of which I didn't know anything before I read about it. Having grown up in Central Europe, I never encountered homosexuality except as an onlooker: we had one or two homosexuals at school who never approached heterosexual boys and, on the other hand, never suffered persecu-tion; they were, in fact, tolerated better than we Jews, for while anti-Semitism preceded Hitler, anti-homosexuality didn't to any-thing like the same extent – and so it was not until I arrived in England, at the age of nineteen, that I learnt that homosexuality was a 'problem'. All of us are emotionally mature in some respects and immature in others, and he would be a daring psychologist who would pronounce Mr Cooper or myself emotionally more mature than Socrates, Plato, Michelangelo, or Leonardo da Vinci; for my part, if I am, I don't want to be, for that kind of superior emotional maturity is nothing to write home about, except as a psychiatric mirage.

But let us pursue Mr Cooper's overt reasoning, his express evidence of Britten's immaturity, his manifest posthumous torture rather than his mere implications or insinuations, to their bitter end. I am not shy, nor 'ill at ease on public occasions', but I cannot for the life of me see that this personality trait makes me (or Mr Cooper, who isn't shy either) emotionally more mature than Britten was, and as for his being 'fully himself only among his close friends', I wonder how fully himself Mr Cooper is with his best enemies. Finally, I knew Benjamin Britten far better than Martin Cooper, but I never noticed any demand for a lifetime of unblemished loyalty; it is, on the contrary, the music critics that demand unblemished loyalty from their colleagues, and what Britten sensitively reacted against was unfavourable criticism of his music, which is where we came in. My personal relationship with Britten was, in fact, marked by the only private, personal row I ever had in my life (whereas my public rows have been legion): at the time of the 1967 Middle East war, he stalked out of our house because I (supported, incidentally, by Deryck Cooke) had opposed his unqualified pacifism; I had asked him what he would have done in place of the Israelis, and when he said that he would have let the Egyptian tanks roll over him, I ventured that he could have taken such a decision as a private individual, but not as Prime Minister of Israel. But our musical friendship remained as close as before; as a mortally sick man, he came to listen to a lecture of mine as well as to the afore-mentioned master class with Peter Pears,* and he inscribed his last major work – the Third String Quartet – to me: the question of loyalty never arose – an interesting comparison, the reader may agree, between historical objectivity and real reality.

Mind you, it seems that you have to be emotionally immature in order to understand children and develop and maintain an 'unspoiled capacity for wonder, for infusing new life and

*See p. 78.

individuality into a familiar situation'. Critical ultra-objectivity means that while, invariably, greatness is gravely flawed, the flaws have their use after all: you have to distribute praise and blame well and wisely, and never mind where they fall, so long as the proportions seem right. In point of fact, they fell rather hard. The implication that the emotionally immature understand children better than the emotionally mature is psychological nonsense; it is immaturity that reacts against children because of its own defences against a threatening childhood that has never been overcome. That certain types of homosexuality make for a love of children is another matter and has nothing to do with immaturity.

As for the capacity for wonder, for infusing new life and individuality into a familiar situation, this surely is one of the most unambiguous signs of genius, from which it would follow that genius, much of it, is a function of immaturity – a deduction which causes Martin Cooper's entire psychological torture to crash-land in absurdity. His fundamental fallacy, a time-honoured one in the critic's view of the world of art, is to let the man explain his music, whereas it is the music that explains the man, shows him at his most developed and characteristic. And the emotional maturity of the music, its insight into the major problems of man, is of a higher order than any critic ever has attained.

It is likely, of course, that had Britten been alive, Martin Cooper's critical torture would still not have been successfully actionable; the main reason why Mr Cooper waited until he was dead was, no doubt, tact. But it is clearly implied in the case I have been putting to the jury that actionable or not, posthumous torture is not a nonsensical concept. *De mortuis nil nisi bene* does not make verifiable sense, but perhaps we can now see that tact towards the dead does, and that it might even contribute to critical sense, whose chief obstacle, destructiveness, it helps to remove.

As transition to the next movement (which, though separated by a double-bar, follows without a break), and aware of the need for both retrospective and prospective thematicism, I propose to ponder the final result of newly-found historical objectivity – found, that is, as Britten had passed into eternity, whence the question arose how to view him *sub-specie æternitatis*. Critical detachment had to be employed, and while at least one foreign writer – H. H. Stuckenschmidt in the *Frankfurter Allgemeine Zeitung* – immediately accorded Britten his proper place in history, Mr Cooper, more practised as a historical critic and also as a historian of criticism, felt the need for critical detachment and caution, alive, perhaps, to the fact that in the past, many a prophet of artistic survival had made a fool of himself. But he overlooked the circumstance that if one did not foresee the future of a great composer, history would not be enthralled by one's wisdom either:

> It would be rash to attempt to forecast the place that Britten will occupy in the history of European music. He was essentially a child of his day, when music had lost its traditional cosmopolitan idiom and composers had to choose between devising an individual dialect of the old language or following the few radicals into unknown territory. Britten's was perhaps the happiest of all the personal idioms achieved, by modifying rather than defying tradition.

I am rash enough to predict, on the basis of what I call analytic evidence, that this negative answer to the question of Britten's future will, as a piece of critical deafness, itself make history, albeit of an unenviable sort. If criticism declines the possibility of assessing enduring substance, what is it there for? *Only* to attempt to destroy? Was I a rash fool when I forecast Schoenberg's place in history? And if I wasn't, how did I do it? Perhaps by preferring, throughout my critical life, analysis to criticism or mere description.

Not that Martin Cooper's critical description and assessment of Britten's art hold water. Britten – like every genius – was essentially not a child of his day: what distinguishes his art is what distinguishes it from every single contemporary trend which, if he used it at all, he used as a background against which he threw his meanings into relief; as a result, and as distinct from the majority of contemporary composers (any age's contemporary composers) he is recognizable within a bar, whereas they, unidentifiable, pass from being contemporary into having been temporary. So estranged did he, in fact, feel from his time, in which he found more than the few radicals which Mr Cooper describes, that his situation in our musical world deeply depressed him. In a gloomy moment, he once murmured that he didn't see much point in going on: if what they produced was music, what was his?

In any case, this entire question of critical assessment, of judgement and evaluation – the last and most burning question of them all, if music criticism is to continue after this book is over – cannot be faced without a clear distinction being drawn between disparate activities which are often and vaguely comprised under the name of music criticism; only thereafter will we have courage to leave the question what to do about it all – unanswered.

2 Description, Analysis and Criticism: A Differential Diagnosis

There is no need to differentiate between an apple and a nipple. Despite more than one level of common characteristics, despite their overlapping connotations, their denotations are worlds apart, and will always remain worlds apart. True, both consist of organic matter. True, both are '-pples' with a vowel preceding. But there's lots of organic matter in this world, and there are lots of '-les', not all of which can etymologically be shown to be diminutives: 'nipple' may, originally, have been one, whereas 'apple' can't. As for the common double 'p', it means as little, i.e. nothing. In short, with all their common traits, the concepts behind the two words can never be mistaken for each other: there'll never be a nipple which anybody will consider an apple, or vice versa.

There is every need in the world to differentiate between schizophrenia and neurosyphilis: to many, their signs and symptoms may seem alike, yet one is a mental state, about which there still is no agreement amongst psychiatrists, whereas the other is a condition due to an infection, about both of which there is total agreement in the medical world. We still don't know whether Schumann suffered from one or the other, but were he alive today, we could demonstrate his syphilis (if any), though we couldn't demonstrate his schizophrenia (if any) – not to, say, Thomas Szasz (a professor of psychiatry), anyway, for whom 'the phenomenon psychiatrists call "schizophrenia" is not a demonstrable medical disease but the name of certain kinds of social deviance (or of behaviour unacceptable to the speaker)'. Current psychiatric attitudes behind the Iron Curtain lend powerful support to Szasz's view: they have produced a 'progressive' state of affairs where, if you are a dissident, you may no longer be imprisoned, but compulsorily committed to a mental hospital instead – for an indefinite period, needless to add, i.e. until you are 'better', whereas a prison sentence at least has an end attached to it. You and I, moreover, would be sharply diagnosable schizophrenics in Soviet Russia – or, at the very least, schizoid personalities: if, despite your intelligence, you don't see, as a matter of course, that the socialist world revolution is the only possible solution to humanity's problems, you must be mad.

Apple and nipple, schizophrenia and neurosyphilis: both pairs are centrally relevant to any attempted differentiation between the description of music, its analysis, and its criticism – otherwise I should not have bothered the reader with my seemingly playful introduction to what is, at this stage in the history of verbal thought about music, the most difficult task of scientific differentiation: yes, don't let's be afraid of the adjective, for if any such differentiation does not attain scientific status, it is hardly worth the attempt.

It is the most difficult task because of the variability of the concepts of description, analysis, and criticism according to the standpoint, the musical and intellectual and indeed historical background of the observer: tell me who you are, musically speaking, and I'll tell you what you mean by description and analysis respectively, and whether you mean anything definable by criticism at all – which, with respect, is doubtful. What is less, I may well be able to tell x that what he means by description is what y means by analysis, and that neither is committing, or need be committing, a fallacy: each may be right from his own standpoint, for you can't either describe or analyse without standing somewhere, and in the current, complex state of the art of listening, it is unlikely that they both stand at exactly the same point.

But however complex, this is, intellectually, the savoury part of the story, whose seamy aspects it would be foolish to deny. Take the transitional tune in the opening movement of Mozart's 'Haffner' Symphony. The propositions, 'This is the second subject' and 'This is not the second subject' have as much in common as the apple and the nipple, though this time it's words instead of letters. Their respective meanings are worlds apart and will always remain worlds apart – and this goes for all equivalent pairs of critical propositions which, in our confused age, are all over the place. In other words, in logical theory, there should be no need to differentiate between the two, yet such is our condition of descriptive, analytic, and critical chaos that the reader will invite me at this stage, with some topical (rather than essential) reason, to differentiate nevertheless.

Well, then, here goes: 'This is the second subject' is wrong description, whereas 'This is not the second subject' is good – or, at the very least, well-implied – analysis. The two propositions, then, have nothing essential in common. 'This is the second subject' confuses theme and key, investing a modulatory tune which starts on the dominant's dominant and ends in the dominant with the significance of a 'subject', just because it's new – in fact, the only new tune in the movement. But there are no modulatory subjects in Mozart, to whom, on the contrary, modulation meant development (which concept should cover the so-miscalled 'bridge passage' too: there are no bridges in good music, which never goes from somewhere to somewhere else across something; good music is always meaningful, between the tunes as well as within them).

'This is not the second subject', on the other hand, is a proposition which draws attention to a fact of supreme analytic significance – Mozart's outright contradiction of normal sonata procedure, to the extent of his inventing a contrasting *tune* that is not a contrasting *subject*, and a contrasting subject – immediately following that tune, and stably in the dominant key – that is not a contrasting tune, but merely inverts the opening, freely and only partly. In short, 'This is the second subject' wrongly describes what the listener can hear anyway, i.e. a new tune, whereas 'This is not the second subject' implies what, maybe, he cannot hear without simultaneous reflection, to wit, that in a structure which depends on the contrast between statement (stable key) and development (modulation), there is no point in calling a modulatory passage a subject, even though it be a tune, for if you do, everything is a subject. So, though there should be no need to differentiate between the two unrelated propositions, I needed all these words to differentiate between them, because while everybody knows what an apple is and what a nipple is, not everybody – not even every professional body – knows what a subject is, or ought to be, if the term is to make consistent sense. If it just meant 'tune', there would be no need for the technical term.

'The finale of Beethoven's Ninth is in free variation form' (an observation all of us have found in innumerable programme notes) and 'The finale of Beethoven's Ninth is a sonata structure accommodating variation' (my own definition, submitted as objective, analytic fact) is a pair of propositions that parallels that juxtaposition of schizophrenia and neurosyphilis. 'Free variation form', that is to say, is not capable of precise explication, because 'normal variation form' isn't either: it depends on what you consider normal, just as schizophrenia depends on what you or the Russians consider normal. When, above, I used the concept of 'free inversion' in my description of the second subject of the 'Haffner' Symphony's first movement, that was a totally different matter: we all know what normal, strict inversion is, in that what's gone up comes down and vice versa, at the identical intervallic distance(s); whereas the 'Haffner's' opening octave inverts into a minor sixth. But 'free variation form', any so-called free variation form, is not, scientifically, a permissible concept: logically and objectively, its connotation and denotation are not definable, and it is invariably used to hide the analyst's or critic's embarrassment at a structure he does not, specifically, understand. Thomas Szasz, likewise, argues that the concept of schizophrenia, in the sense(s) in which we use it, is not permissible.

But permissible or not, into which category of conceptual, verbalized reactions to music does this 'free variation form' of Beethoven's choral finale fall? It is a critical description. We have to regard it as descriptive rather than analytic because once again, it merely points to what one can hear anyway, i.e. variations; but it is criticism at the same time because the verdict 'free', however meaningless objectively, implies judgement. Variations, that is, exist without an evaluating witness, but freedom doesn't, because the notion stands or falls with evaluative standards of strictness.

The 'sonata structure accommodating variations', on the other hand, is, in my submission, as objectively analytical an observation as is the diagnosis of neurosyphilis: it identifies what causes the music to be what it is, and defines what are the exact determinants of what one hears and experiences as being musically logical. The background is, in fact, sonata form, if we accept that in tonal music, the form is based on an extended integration of two types of contrast – the contrast of themes and/or keys, and the aforementioned (but, otherwise, never-mentioned) contrast between statement and development. In a well-definable way, in fact, this choral finale is a more explicit sonata structure than many a more conventional one, rubs in the sonata's all-important exposition far more emphatically than does any sonata layout that does not include a repeat of the exposition – a device which is designed, above all, to serve memorability: what is going to be developed has to be remembered in the first place.

Prototypically, Beethoven had omitted the repeat of the exposition in the first movement of his String Quartet in F major, Op. 59 No. 1. With this characteristically impatient step, he had actually jumped a natural stage in the development of musical composition, in which repetition can normally be seen to grow into, and be replaced by variation. The varied exposition instead of the repeated exposition would, in fact, have been the next logical step, but owing to Beethoven's forward-urging genius, it never happened – except in a genre whose texture persuaded composers to construct a double exposition, i.e. in the classical concerto, where the solo exposition emerges as a variation – a 'developing variation', as Schoenberg would say – of the tutti exposition. Otherwise, speaking a little more precisely, it *almost* never happened. In our own century, very late indeed in the history of the Austro-German sonata, an Englishman made up for the Austro-Germans' omission of this compositorial stage in one single work: in the first movement of his Second, C major String Quartet, Benjamin Britten succeeds a highly compressed first exposition by an extended and varying second round of exposing his themes before he plunges into his development section.

And Beethoven himself, in the choral finale, seems to be making inspired amends for his equally inspired impatience, for he does in fact write a double exposition, the first instrumental, and modulating to the dominant as of old – whence the seeming return to the opening leads, in fact, to the second, varied, vocal exposition. Heard in this light, the variations lose their 'freedom' (whatever that may have amounted to) and take their natural place in the sonata build-up. I thus submit that the proposition, 'The finale of Beethoven's Ninth is a sonata structure accommodating variation' is uncritical analysis: judgement does not come into it so long as we agree on the nature of sonata and the nature of variation, any variation.

It would, however, be facile simply to suggest that while criticism is judgement, analysis is about what can't be heard unaided, and description about what can. I have intimated that it all depends on the standpoint, but the trouble is, or rather the troubles are, that at least two different standpoints have to be taken into account, the speaker's or writer's and the addressees, and that these standpoints must needs vary along a system of co-ordinates one of which marks the personality and musicality of the person in question, the other his position in the history of composition and/or the history of listening: the situation is as complicated as that. If it weren't, the need to differentiate between description, analysis and criticism could never arise.

What was analysis to Mozart (even though he did not know the term) is description to us – anything he said about his own music. And what is analysis to us, or to the more developed musicians amongst us, was a secret to him, which he entirely kept to himself – not perhaps because he wanted to, but because he had no choice: nobody would have known what he was talking about, not even his father; nor indeed was he affected by the need for verbalization – which, in the nineteenth century, emerged as an anxiety symptom in proportion as our general musical language began to break up.

Wagner showed this need in no uncertain measure; he and Brahms can, perhaps, be described as the first analysts in our sense. It is especially since the publication of the first volume of Cosima Wagner's diaries* that we realize how 'modern' Wagner's analytic mind was. Cosima noted down all his analytic observations, and quite often the reader is under the impression that he is perusing the diaries of Mrs Schoenberg or, at the very least, the diaries of Mrs Pfitzner. What we tend to call description, on the other hand, i.e. that which you can hear anyway, plays virtually no role in Wagner's reflections on music – whereas judgement, criticism, pervade his analyses: he analyses in order to justify his criticisms, be they favourable or unfavourable – though he takes far greater care to substantiate positive reactions (to Bach and, of course, Beethoven above all).

But if Mozart's analyses are descriptions to 'us', who are we? Where does the differentiation remain now between people, between personalities and indeed degrees and types of musicality? 'We' are, needless to add, you and I, but what about the others, of whom there are also a few? As a matter of fact, there are more of the others than there used to be, far more than there used to be in Mozart's time – a circumstance which gives rise to a paradox that further confounds our attempts at a workable differential diagnosis. In Mozart's time, that is to say, music lovers were musical. I am not implying that all potentially musical people were music lovers: many may not have had the opportunity to grow up with, and into

*See pp. 96–7.

music, especially if they did not happen to live in the right social context. But those who loved music understood it – understood it instinctively, emotionally, and there is no musical understanding without this instinctive basis, anyway. Owing to their instinctive and, accordingly, confident approach to music, they were not in need of either analysis or description; indeed, in the main, Mozart himself considered his analytic or descriptive observations his private business – a family affair: he made them to his father.

But he regarded them as all the more important for being private, otherwise he would not have made them at all. To us – to you and me, that is to say – they often seem quite naïve, if we are honest enough to overcome what is, after all, our *justified* awe in the face of anything that Mozart cared to say. It is not easy to accept the demonstrable fact that even God can make a mistake or, at least, can be naïve: only atheists accept that fact with gleeful ease, and by definition, they can hardly claim to be experts on the workings of God's mind.

Realizing that Mozart could be verbally naïve about music is not, however, good enough. You and I cannot hope even to get within tritonic distance – as near, at least, as F sharp major is to C major – of Mozart's complex, indeed all-embracing musico-psychological sophistication, so what the hell makes him analytically or descriptively naïve, conceptually tautological, what makes him attach the same analytic weight to his descriptions as the Russian psychiatrists attach to 'their' schizophrenia, which is, in fact, your normal mental state and mine?

The answer is – conceptualization, verbalization, which, for Mozart, was an intellectual luxury, aesthetically superfluous and, for this very reason, a psychological achievement, an 'extra', a bonus: he had bothered to translate the untranslatable.

Now, in our own time, there are, as I have tried to indicate, plenty of people apart from you and me, plenty of people who love music nevertheless. There are, in fact, not only plenty of unmusical music lovers, but even plenty of unmusical performers and, yes, plenty of unmusical composers: John Cage, whose palpably artistic and original mind has to be treated with respect, is a paradigm, in that between ourselves, you and I should describe him as provably unmusical. Even Pierre Boulez, *pace* his truly fantastic ear, is incapable of hearing harmonic rhythm as you and I instinctively know it – does not, in fact, know what a phrase is, and has never phrased anything in his life, all the less so since his own music (impressive in other dimensions) doesn't stand in need of phrasing anyway.

The disintegration of our general musical language, together with the disappearance of common ideals (pre-eminently religious aims), has produced a state of mental affairs in which music can easily be good for the soul – the listener's, player's, composer's – even though you and I may regard the soul in question as jolly unmusical, or, at the inside, as defectively musical. And this is the point, the precise stage in the development or (as you and I should say) the envelopment of western musicality, where the paradox explodes: Mozart was too musical to see the naïvety, the tautology of his verbal reactions to his own music, whereas many a contemporary listening mind is too unmusical to see equivalent descriptions of music for what they are, and hence proceeds to regard them as analyses, since the music's meaning did not, specifically, get across in the first place. Mozart was too musical to ignore descriptions by the *strange word*; many of our time's listening minds are too unmusical to ignore descriptions of *strange music*. And while Mozart's music lover was not remotely as musical as Mozart, he was not remotely as unmusical as many a contemporary composer of ours, not to speak of a large proportion of our own music lovers. Inasmuch as they don't hear what's going on, they regard description as analysis, and analysis as musicology, for which special knowledge is required – whereas all you need to know in order to understand analysis is the music itself, of which you have to have had a genuine experience in the first place.

Compared to this Gordian knot of confusion between description and analysis – let alone criticism itself, to which, nowadays, the functions of either are readily attributed – any R. D. Laingian knots are downright sonatinas, and before we know where we are, we shall, after all, have to distinguish between an apple and a nipple, lest even the difference between these two might be thought to be of minor importance – a matter for obsessionally pedantic logicians who have too few real worries.

It follows that we have to know where we are. Fundamentally, that is, intellectual life is simple: even *The Critique of Pure Reason* is, once you are prepared not to cloud its basic issue with your own preoccupations – the issue between what Kant called the appearance and the thing in itself. And the basic issue before us at this point is, plainly, that of musicality *versus* unmusicality in our time. Just as it would be impossible for a gifted twentieth-century composer to create in the style of Mozart, so it is impossible for a musical twentieth-century recipient to listen in the style of Mozart and his music lovers. Musical experience has become more self-conscious, or simply more conscious, for those who are capable of it at all; in fact, all experience has. We have arrived at the tail-end of a culture which, as all of us – conservatives as well as progressives – are aware, is overlapping with a new one whose outlines are, as yet, barely visible, and the friction between the two cannot but produce a powerful counter-force against naïvety which, if we recognize it at all, we perceive, according to temperament, either as stupidity or as a lost paradise. The intensely musical person of today, whoever he is, is not naïvely musical: he feels the urge to justify his musical experience – even, if he is a composer, his creative experience – at least to himself. The weakly musical, or the unmusical music lover may feel the same urge, but the all-important difference is that while he will proceed to justify his experiences either extra-musically (say, politically) or tautologically ('Ah! this is the second subject!' – as if naming it changed the intellectual situation and proved him more clever than poor old Mozart was, who didn't even know the term), the intensely musical person will want to justify musically – by analysis, which looks for the why behind the how.

Our variables, then – different people, different musicalities, different times – are sufficiently reducible to constants to make our hoped-for differentiations possible after all, even though we cannot hope that everybody will understand, and thus agree with us; but then, we cannot hope, either, that everybody will understand the music which is being described, analysed, and/or criticized. The days are long past, at this end of our culture, when people were only open to what, potentially, they could understand, and our mass medias' compulsion about universal accessibility is a logical response to the enthusiastic abolition of the difference between stupidity and intelligence, between untalent and talent, that seems to be one of the driving forces, or rather, one of the braking forces, of our dying civilization, which only the most courageous intellects and hearts can face surviving.

Very closely in this connection, a little controversy I had with my supreme boss, the Director-General of the BBC, will throw my point – the proper starting-point for our attempted differential diagnosis – into clear relief. He had given a speech upon the occasion of the fortieth anniversary of our Audience Research, which was reported and quoted in our house journal, *Ariel*, on 20 October, 1976. I responded with a letter to the Editor, published on 17 November:

> In reply to D.G.'s autobiographical observation that he 'would rather be plebeian and effective than élitist and ignored', I should rather be neither, and would resign if I were either. But I'd rather feel obliged to people who are interested in my programmes than to people who aren't – whence I prefer meeting the demands of a small, vital audience to boring its pants off by trying to interest those who aren't really interested, and thus increasing my total audience.
>
> Successful communication is not just 'effective', but truthful to its substance and faithful to its self-elected addressees. We are neither priests nor politicians, and are, thank God, in no position to tell people what's good for them.

Ariel appended the Director-General's rejoinder: 'Hans is following his usual élitist line, disregarding the context of my observation, as well as the fact that broadcasting is a mass medium, however he seeks to frustrate it.'

I am not here concerned with the occasion of the controversy nor indeed with its substance, but solely with its symptomatic significance: élitism is a concept which was invented as recently as a decade or two ago, an emotive, derogatory, pseudo-democratic, almost psychotic denial of the fact that all men are not equal. If a substantial proportion of the population were colour-blind, it would be élitist to talk about colour, not to speak of analysing a painting and its colour scheme.

In this sense, and in this sense only, I propose to adopt an 'élitist' point of view when getting down to my differentiation: I shall try to define, in the first place, what description means to you and me, then what analysis should mean to us and, finally, where (if anywhere) criticism comes in.

The prototype of description is the programme note we never read: if we know the music, we don't need it, and if we don't, we don't want it. Not only do we find verbal anticipation of what we are going to hear painful, if not indeed an insult to our perceptivity, but it is inevitable for all verbal descriptions of music to be selective and proportionately misleading. Just as the television camera replaces our well-motivated eye in focusing our attention on what the

producer happens to choose for close inspection, so the
programme-noter picks and chooses and ignores according to his
predilections, his current preoccupations, and the pre-selectors
from whom he cribs.

   Contrary to scholarly beliefs, two of them, according to which
criticism is a department of analysis or, alternatively, analysis is a
department of criticism, it is, in fact, simple description that tends
to incorporate criticism to a far greater extent than does any analysis. What is worse, while criticism is overt when analysis incorporates it, or when it incorporates analysis, the criticism that hides
inside description is the most pernicious of the lot – *creeping criticism*, which is as malignant as it is unconfessed, even un-self-
confessed.

   I am not, of course, thinking of all that simple-eared propaganda
which descriptions contain as a direct result of the writer not
knowing what, precisely, to say next: 'A beautifully lyrical second
subject forms a stark contrast to the sharply rhythmical, but none
the less impressive first, which opens the body of the movement
(allegro) after a slow and introspective introduction (adagio) from
which this rhythmical theme emerges, gradually and, at first, hesit-
antly.' That's all right for anybody who wishes to see his superficial
perceptions confirmed, or pre-confirmed, in print – and if there
weren't plenty of those, the newspapers themselves would be out
of business, or else change into news-sheets.

   What I mean by creeping criticism is the noise dozens of des-
cribers – depressing that I am the first to use this noun in our
present context, isn't it? – make about, say, the first movement of
the 'Haffner' Symphony being monothematic, since the second
subject is (obviously) based upon the first. But that contrasting
transitional tune I have discussed they don't mention at all –
because it doesn't fit into their would-be analytic scheme of things,
which, at this stage in the history of 'informed' criticism (informed
by Schoenberg, Reti, and myself, or rather misinformed, the 'mis-'
part lying in the ear of the beholder, not the informing agents),
exalts monothematicism, hidden or blatant, into original virtue: a
subtle symptom, this, of our disintegrating culture, which is preoccupied with unity as none before.

   In other (but not surprisingly different) words, this kind of
ruthless description of the 'Haffner's' opening movement, though
there is nothing wrong with it so far as it goes, represents creeping

evaluation by dint of its choice of structural topics, determined as the describer is not to go far enough to include the contrasting, transitional tune as a central topic of, at least, descriptive observation. At the same time, it is that very tune, on the surface the only bit in the entire movement which is not thematic, which is, for this very reason, the only melody worth talking about: how does it fit in, and what is the reason for thus splitting the functions of the second subject – its harmonic function and its thematic function? This is a strictly analytic question which descriptive, creeping evaluation prevents us from attempting to answer.

The analyst, aware of the fact that his reply would be an evaluation too, a verdict that unity obtains (which, though it does nowise guarantee value, is a *conditio sine qua non* of sense), would make it his sacred aesthetic duty to answer these two questions. First, how does the tune fit in? Easy, if you have had an instinctive understanding of the structure before any attempt at analysis – and if you haven't had it, no such attempt is legitimate, justifiable artistically. The background line of the first subject is D–C$\sharp$–B–A, descending: tonic to dominant, in conjunct motion. Now, the background line of the transitional tune is F$\sharp$–E–D–C$\sharp$: again a perfect fourth, submediant to mediant, descending in conjunct motion – within the framework of the key about to be established, the second-subject (dominant) key. In short, the relation between the first subject and the transitional tune develops on the basis of what I have called the principle of the postponed consequent: the background line of the new tune's basic entity is, in fact, a simple sequence of the model that is the background of the opening of the movement.

And why does Mozart do it? In order meaningfully to contradict expectations – the expectation of a second subject that would be a new tune in the dominant key, and the expectation of an unmelodic or less-than-melodic transition which draws its manifest material, its foreground material, from what has gone before. Such logical contradiction of equally logical – i.e. well-implied – expectation is all that musical meaning is about, and it is a lot: unspeakable, unverbalizable psychological truths are thus discovered and unmistakably conveyed.

The difference between description and analysis is now crystallizing: it seems to depend, to an unexpected extent, on the drastically different roles which criticism plays in either. Metaphorically speaking, description concerns itself with the journey through a

work and its emotional content: at best, at its least harmful, it
behaves like a travel guide; whereas analysis is concerned with
(and, when emphatically critical, about) the journey's reason, purpose, and practicality, its sheer desirability and, of course, the
particular mode of travel that might be recommended. At its most
critical, that is, analysis takes over the duties of a travel agent, take
him or leave him. Many people prefer to travel without such
advice.

But most people in their senses prefer to travel without a travel
guide, for the same reason as many people prefer, or should prefer,
opera without television – because they object to having the beauty
spots picked and, by implication, evaluated for them. It is for me,
and me alone, to decide what I want to concentrate on or even
confine my attention to – or else, preferably, what I want to take in
contrapuntally as it were, comprehensively, with equal attention
devoted to everything, as if each thing were receiving exclusive
attention: this, after all, is the unique miracle of musical (as opposed
to conceptual) cognition – its comprehensiveness, which the creeping criticism of description utterly destroys. In our own time,
musical perception, the power of concentration and the quality of
listening, can be shown to have degenerated in proportion as description has gained the upper hand – not only in programme notes,
books, and (often learned) articles, but also in musical education,
which is becoming ever more descriptive as it adjusts to the
methods of the mass media.

I sincerely hope I shall not sound self-preoccupied or conceited
when I propose that the purest differential diagnosis between description and analysis is provided by functional analysis – my own
wordless method of analysing: I compose analytic scores, which are
played together with the works they analyse, without a word being
spoken or read. On the lecture tour in Canada which included the
previously-mentioned symposium on music criticism at Mc-
Master's,* I not only lectured but had one or two analyses played in
my presence. It must be remembered that when they are broadcast,
I cannot observe their effect on audiences and cannot get many
listeners' reactions, but in Canada I had wide-ranging opportunities
to see and sense how such analytic communications get across not
only to musicians, but also to the most important listener of all, the

---

*See pp. 33–4.

'ordinary music lover'. Dreadful phrase: he could not be less ordinary, for it is, after all, to him that music is addressed in the first place, not to the professionally prejudiced and preoccupied, who himself all too easily gives in to the doubtful joys of description – even though the only descriptions he likes are usually his own.

Now, one of the chief reasons why I introduced this wordless method was precisely in order to get rid altogether of description, which is why I here offer it as the best source of differential diagnosis: you can't describe music musically, though you can describe music verbally, and words, like Zarathustra's, musically. What gratified me in Canada was the relief people felt in aural view of the death of description; previously, I had only experienced three proper public performances of my analyses, one at Hampstead Town Hall, one at the Aldeburgh Festival, where Benjamin Britten expressed the same relief, and one in Jerusalem – where, needless to add, everybody developed the method further and improved it at question time. Otherwise, all performances have been by radio organizations, and reactions to such broadcasts come, in the main, from the profession.

What, then, does my method analyse? The unity of contrasts – which is what, ultimately, all analysis is, or should be about, for the simple reason that everything else is, in principle, audible to the naked ear. But the background unity of contrasting motifs, phrases, themes, rhythms, harmonies, movements, requires analytic (i.e. ultimately self-analytic) investigation, unless the contrasts are so weak that the unity is in the foreground of the music, and the music itself, accordingly, boring. Of course, the elucidation of the structural function of whatever one hears in the course of a composition is part and parcel of the unearthing of the music's unifying elements.

The role of criticism in functional analysis, or in any kind of factual analysis, has always been overestimated, because the human mind finds it difficult not to judge. Unity does not show value; it shows the possibility of value. *Bolero* evinces total unity, but is not a great masterpiece; on the contrary, the composer was aware of writing a piece of non-communicative music, of hypnosis. More than one Bruckner symphony, on the other hand, lacks complete unity without lacking supreme genius. By implication, the analytic establishment of unity does, of course, praise – but only to the extent of saying: other things being equal, it is better – clearer, more logical, more economic – for this unity to obtain. Since, however, other things are never equal in works of artistic substance, identical as they frequently are in the schoolroom, analysis can never produce a basis for comparative evaluation, except again in the schoolroom, or after a multi-dimensionally complete analysis of the works that are being compared.

Thus faced frontally, the problems of criticism, of judgement, are immense when compared to the tedious difficulties of description and the fascinating problems of analysis. Nor have I, in my differential diagnosis, yet touched upon the ultimate problem of criticism, which is: why should we criticize anyway? Description elicits nothing; analysis elicits facts, truths, promotes understanding – even promotes evaluation, but such promotion cannot be regarded as evaluation's *raison d'être*: plenty of worthy activities yield useless or even harmful side-products and side-effects. The fact is that the justification of criticism in its purest – evaluative – sense has never been seriously challenged.

3 The Twilight of the Critics
(*Kritikerdämmerung*)

At the end of the section before last, under a clouded sky which seemed to contradict the weather forecast implicit in my Preface, I made quite a cannibalistic meal of Martin Cooper's obituary piece on Benjamin Britten – for five reasons. First, a leading critic's summing-up of a leading composer's creative and extra-creative life is destined to assume a significance, positive or negative, that far transcends its topicality. Secondly, the piece is truly representative – of the phoniness and the destructive quality of both unfavourable and would-be objective criticism. From this point of view, I could, of course, have chosen hundreds of other criticisms, but what made me humourlessly enthusiastic about picking this one was, thirdly, my passion for professional (as distinct from personal!) disloyalty: here was a much-respected friend and colleague whose notice, nevertheless, had to be torn to shreds in defence of our art. A simple enough consideration, this, once you free yourself of etiquette and professional protocol and decide upon a course of elementary decency and fairness instead – decency towards both people and their work, and there is no decency without realism and, yet more important, no realism without decency: there is no truth worth knowing that does not impose moral obligations, and no morality, of course, that is heedless of truth, some tiny but relevant bit of it, at least.

Fourthly and frankly, Britten as the 'child of his time', coming from a critic, was too much absurdity to bear: it is the critic who, prototypically, is the child of his time and, trying to pull himself out of it by his own bootlaces, plunges the artist into it – the very man whose function it is to create out of contemporary waters, though it will always be refreshing, in a chilling way, to go for a swim.

Fifthly and above all, inasmuch as Martin Cooper's piece professes to offer objective, historical description, it is full of creeping criticism, to which pursuit he does, in fact, give a new twist, in that the music's virtues are used to highlight the man's defects – as if the man's defects, real or imaginary, were a proper subject for a critic of the arts at all: we know what happened to reality when the phoney profession of psychiatry got hold of the arts and turned them into its material, into an acceptable replacement for neurosis or even psychosis.

But then, what is the proper pursuit of criticism, once it is divested of sheer description and separated from analysis? Indeed, the question I posed at the end of the last section was in no way facetious, flippant, facile: it is a grave question once a not so tiny bit of truth is accepted, one which has been concealed by a conspiracy of silence throughout the history of music criticism as a profession – that the discipline has done untold harm and hurt to many of those criticized. See for yourself; meet them, ask them – and the conspiracy of silence will frighten you, because you will come to realize that it is the critic's victims, too, that are responsible for the story of unsensational suffering remaining untold, for without their connivance, it would have been told over and over again. Nor is it out of respect for criticism or the critics that the victims have remained silent; rather, it is out of ill-conceived self-respect, out of obedience to a conventionalized command that is none the less effective for having remained unwritten, often unarticulated even – that one must be able to take criticism, that one must not reply, protest, or justify oneself. As one who, wisely or not, is so little concerned, or has learnt to be so little concerned, about what is being written about him that he is the only writer he knows who has not subscribed to a press-cutting agency, without at the same time refusing to read reviews of his misdeeds when they happen to come his way, I am, perhaps, within my intellectual and ethical rights to again ask, in utter amazement: why has one to be able to take criticism? Why should one not respond to it? If the ultimate aim is truth, and if the criticism in question is a lie, or a mistake, or an illusion, could it not be said with better reason that it is one's duty to hit back, with the force of truth engaging the power of the critic? It would, at the very least, be an interesting combat, fascinating for power-seekers and truth-seekers alike, as well as for those, the majority alas, who are a bit of both.

For it is, in the last resort, the music critic's power that has produced the conspiracy of silence, the meek acceptance of the situation by the musician. I am not talking about professionally effective power which, in fact, I believe to be vastly, paranoically overrated, at any rate in Britain, though the constellation of influences may be different in the United States. But in our country, it is decidedly untrue to say that the critic can 'make or break' an artist; in close on two decades in the Music Department of the BBC, for instance, I have never seen anybody, any producer or more senior officer, take the slightest interest in what a critic had to say about the quality of a composer's or performer's work, and I know I am not alone in committing newspaper cuttings sent along by agents or publishers straight to the wastepaper basket.

No, the power I am talking about is of a less tangible, but none the less sinister and effective kind: it is the power, the black magic, of the printed word, which lends authority where there is no authority, interest where there is no interest, power where there is no force. If the music critic wrote his notices in the form of letters to his readers, it is doubtful whether they would ever get to the end of them. But once the critic's thoughts see the dark of print, he has no difficulty at all in establishing the phoney professional's divine right always to know better. But as distinct from the other phoney professions, music criticism is in an extreme position, for while the critic is being paid and read for invariably knowing better, he almost invariably knows worse: few are the music critics whose sheer competence matches that of their victims, because if it did, they probably would not remain mere critics.

From both his editor's and the public's point of view, however, it is the critic's duty to know better, as a result of which he is likely to suffer total moral corruption: innumerable are the occasions where, if he were honest, he would have to say, 'I don't know', 'I don't really understand', 'I can't judge because this is not my kind of music', but he never says it, for this is not what he is being paid for, financially by his editor, and psychologically by himself – in terms of the vapid self-respect of the phoney professional who depends for the esteem in which he is being held on the authority of his position and the conventionality of the execution of his task.

Owing to the conspiracy of silence, the music critic's authority easily is, in effect, dictatorial, because it is unchallengeable unless his editor sacks him, and his editor, a phoney professional himself, is likely to sack him for the wrong reasons, if at all: just imagine if I returned to newspaper criticism and started having a go at my fellow critics, challenging their authority with good musical reason – I'd be sacked tomorrow.

The questions, 'Why should we criticize?' and 'What is the proper pursuit of criticism?' assume weighty significance when considered in the light, if light is the word, of the critic's unchallengeable authority. From the critical profession itself, the two questions usually receive a collective, a lump answer – to the effect that criticism is the life-blood of intellectual and artistic development, discourse, and intercourse, and that without criticism, which distinguishes between good and bad or tries to, anyway, the artist would be in an authoritarian position, imposing his work on an uncritical audience.

It is a neat projection of the critic's own authoritarianism, which has proved astoundingly successful, considering that it is not very clever. For where is this intellectual or aesthetic intercourse or discourse? The very function of criticism, in this sense, depends on its challengeability: criticism that is not criticizeable is not criticism, but the issuing of an unfavourable or, for that matter, favourable edict. It's no good making a democratic gesture towards the artist, speaking to him on behalf of that imaginary entity, the people, if the first thing you resent is anybody addressing you on behalf of all those who disagree with you. Martin Cooper, it will be remembered,* alluded to Britten's sensitivity to criticism, which he considered emotionally immature – but Britten was downright thick-skinned *vis-à-vis* his critics when you compared his dismay to their own sensitivity to their critic, namely, my humble self – and I was, naturally, in a perfect position to compare.

For our own purposes, in any event, we had better keep the two questions about the justification and the nature of criticism apart: our answers are likely to be pessimistic, and it would not be fair to deal out, by way of repayment, a lump sum of pessimism. Indeed, both pessimism and optimism have to be substantiated rather more rigorously than views without evaluative involvement, whose sole basis is observation, which is its own substantiation.

Why should we criticize at all, then – assuming for the sake of the fairest possible argument, that our public criticisms were challengeable, or that a convention could be allowed to develop within

---

*See p. 129.

which criticism actually asked for counter-criticism? I submit that even in that case, the question does not altogether lose its rhetorical element – not from the artistic point of view, anyway. For can we honestly say that if all music criticism stopped tomorrow, the art of music would be the loser? Is there any historical evidence which would entitle us to say yes? Can we find any negative criticism in the history of criticism, no matter whether it was submitted by an exclusive critic or a composer-critic, which can be shown to have assisted the development of our art? Positive criticisms, yes, like Schumann's of Chopin, but would we ever agree to confine music criticism to favourable reactions, and have not, down the centuries, unfavourable reactions proved far more harmful than the odd inspired favourable reaction (usually by a composer-critic) has proved useful? Art can, in fact, look after itself.

Nor indeed is the assumption that you have to learn to 'listen critically', to discriminate and distinguish between good and bad, artistically tenable. For owing to that conspiracy of silence which has produced a refusal to question the very basis of institutionalized criticism, the most important artistic secret has never been made public – that mediocre artists apart, the artist does not aim to produce something good, and should not be expected to do so. The student should, until he attains testable mastery. Thenceforth, 'goodness', if any meaning can be distilled from the concept at all, turns from an end into a means of saying something new and true and making it clear and as short as possible in the circumstances; it is significant that we only allow the noun 'goodness' in the ethical sphere, as does the German language (*Güte*). It has been forced into the world of art by the compulsion to evaluate, itself originally a moralizing need. The critic is, of course, the logical consequence, end result, and representative of this compulsion, but that doesn't make him good; it only makes him a continual, warning sign of our own weakness, which we ignore not only at our own peril, unfortunately, but also the artist's.

I have, in fact, always listened as uncritically as possible, especially to begin with, at the very moment when, in view of something new, the critic is expected to employ his critical capacities to the utmost. But at the outset, one has to discover what the artist has to say or is trying to say; how can we judge how he is saying it if we don't know what it is?

Though we have not found the answer to the first question,

why, from an artistic point of view, we should criticize at all, we have prepared the ground for the answer to the second, about the proper pursuit of music criticism, if music criticism there is to be. Since music is an unconceptual art, conceptual explanation is impossible. But it is possible, nevertheless, to point to the arrival of something new and true, even in performance – for without the performer conveying something new, what do we need a new performer for, or a new performance by an old performer? Let us always play the same gramophone record and have done with it – of the same work too, so long as it is 'good': why expose ourselves to new risks of badness?

Once we have a clear knowledge of what the artist has to say, it is, of course, possible to judge where he – composer or performer – fails in saying it, though in the case of the composer, we shall hardly be able to do so after the first performance of a work – at the very moment when the critic is expected to reach a crucial stage in the pursuit of his craft. It is unlikely, in any case, that he will be able to judge how something is said without understanding why it is said, why one thing follows, or doesn't follow, from another. The conclusion seems inescapable that the proper pursuit of criticism is hardly possible without analysis – and if, in the end, analysis usurps criticism, as it has done in the case of the present writer, so much the better: the dangers of criticism exposed in this book are thus avoided, and the analyst does, in fact, find himself living by implied praise alone, even though mistakes are analysable. But who wants to analyse them unless he is paid for it (as a teacher), where there is an infinite amount of great substance to analyse and thus reflect upon?

But since criticism seems as unavoidable as war, and for much the same reasons, the necessity to humanize it by analysis must always be uppermost in our minds. In case the typical music critic finds my comparison a little far-fetched, let me show him that it could not have been fetched from closer by: like the critic, the person or nation that wages war invariably does it for the ultimate good of the vicitim and, beyond that, of humanity, and it is only the victim who feels victimized. The fact of the ethical case is, of course, that it is for the victim, the artist, to decide what is good for him,* if not indeed for those whom he addresses, so far as the

---

*Cf. the end of my letter about broadcasting on p. 143.

furtherance of comprehension of what he has to say is concerned –
in which context I may be forgiven if I find it significant that within
the musical profession, it has been the composers rather than the
critics who have welcomed my wordless method of musical analysis with open arms. Britten was chief amongst them and commissioned such a functional analysis of Mozart's last string quartet for
performance at his festival; when, at question time, an eminently
spiritual lady got up and said that for her, the analysis destroyed the
poetry of the work, Britten, unaggressive in public as he normally
was, got up in his turn and said that for him, the analysis added to
the poetry.

That, of course, was either an exaggeration or an illusion, for an
analysis cannot contain anything the work itself does not contain,
but it can illuminate its poetry, and any poetry that has to shun the
sunlight of illumination is not worth its oft-misused name.

Wordless or not, analysis cannot but be helped by a recognition
of the laws of musical thought, and of the way in which they
operate in order to produce musical logic, one thing following
from another. We have described the laws,* but not their operation. When we said that all meaningful music depended on them,
we did not add the rider that all meaningless music didn't. Now,
the background of a composition – the sum total of its implied
expectations – is, in itself, meaningless, in that nothing happens in
it that cannot be supplied by the expectant listener if he just proceeds to meet his expectations: the composer is no longer necessary. In the furthest background, all is repetition, total unity, which
is why Bolero† is a deliberate piece of non-music, hypnosis and
stimulation (for hypnosis can both stimulate and send to sleep)
rather than communication. In this remote background, therefore,
pre-musical as it were, the laws of conceptual thought do still
obtain because music hasn't started thinking: a thing, a phrase, is
still itself and remains itself – nothing happens to it, because all you
expect to happen is repetition. In our musical culture, the prototype
is the ostinato without, if I may so put it, anything to be obstinate
about, or a basis without anything on top of it. There are such
compositions, sheer background without foreground, especially in
our own time, within the Cage-inspired school of endless repeti-

*See p. 115.
†Cf. p. 147.

tion. In them, the laws of musical thought do not operate, whereas the laws of conceptual thought apply: in this sense, they are the most unmusical thing imaginable.

Musical things begin to happen when the composer's creativity sets to work on such a background and he, instinctively, piles level upon level, backgrounds ever closer to the front, or else, more usually, avails himself of multi-levelled backgrounds put at his disposal by his musical culture, until he reaches the foreground of his work, his individual invention, which follows the laws of musical thought by not letting anything remain itself, by producing diversity and contrasts out of the original, wholly unitarian idea.

Now, the way in which the laws of musical thought here operate, the laws to which they themselves are subject, or rather subjected – as the laws of conceptual thought are subjected to the laws of deductive and inductive reasoning – are not obscure either, and should have struck those who are psychoanalytically versed half a century ago – except that, unfortunately, musical understanding and psychological understanding do not always seem to go together as happily as music and medicine, or music and mathematics. For the mechanisms employed to turn background into foreground are exactly the same as those which distinguish the Freudian 'primary process' – the laws of *unconscious* pictorial thought which are sharply opposed to what happens in our minds consciously, by way of the 'secondary process'. In the primary process it is the processes of 'displacement', 'condensation', and 'representation through the opposite' that rule mental events, as can be seen in the formation of the manifest dream out of the latent dream content. The identical processes distinguish the way in which the laws of musical thought operate, except that they are not condemned to unconsciousness and are, instead, formalized, legalized, according to the accepted conventions of the musical culture within which they are happening – though these conventions can themselves, in due course, be pushed into the background and be meaningfully contradicted by the foreground, by new, newly formalized applications of the primary process.

What, in any case, makes the tensions so created between foreground and background demonstrably meaningful is the combination of maximal contrast and maximal unity between them: the higher the maxima, the greater the tension, the greater the meaning.

A perfect and complete cadence in the tonic, once it has happened, doesn't leave any tension, but then it doesn't leave any meaning either, except that something has come to an end, for the purpose of which signal the background – the fulfilled expectation – has come fully to the fore: all meaning spent, there is no more to be said. An interrupted cadence, on the other hand, though by now fairly conventionalized and thus capable of being treated as a background itself (roughly since Wagner), combines maximal unity between itself and its background with maximal contradiction: the chord on the submediant shares two of its three notes (its mediant and its dominant) with the expected tonic triad, while its most important note, the root and bass, has been displaced, producing the Freudian 'displacement of affect', extremely drastically so. At the same time, the displacement heeds harmonic conventions: the leading-note still leads to the tonic, and the dominant seventh (if any) to the mediant; it is, after all, these conventions which help to create the expectation of the tonic chord.

Again and again, I have chosen this interrupted cadence as a paradigm of what my entire theory of music is about – for the simple reason that within two chords, all my postulates about the relation between foreground and background are supported by hard, clear evidence which does not seem to admit of any other explanation.

Not that my description of the laws to which the laws of musical thought are subjected – those of the formalized and legitimized primary process – has to remain at all hypothetical anyway: fortunately, thoughtful music does not rest content with employing silent backgrounds but, especially in extended structures, makes use of sounding backgrounds as well. In sonata form, above all, the all-important first stage of the structure, the at first repeated, later unrepeated (but rarely varied) exposition,* serves as a demonstrable background for the development section and also, in the more evolved varieties of the species, for the recapitulation. It is here, therefore, that the operation of displacement, condensation, and representation through the opposite can simply be observed, without the need for a working hypothesis surviving the initial results of one's investigations. But while sonata form – the most complex instrumental form in western music – gives one the fullest possible picture of the way in which the laws of musical thought operate,

---

*Cf. pp. 137–8.

there are other forms, too, in which a sounding background enables one to study the precise relation between foreground and background without any theorizing intervening; in variation form, for instance, so long as it isn't purely and boringly ornamental and decorative, the theme is a clear background to the contradicting foreground of the variations – some of them, anyway.

It remains to be added, at the risk of being suspected of granting the performer unmusicological licence, that he, too, has his background to work upon – the score. If this were not so, a definitive electronic performance could soon replace the performer's efforts altogether. Of course, he has to remain well within the composer's prescriptions – or so it seems to the critical ear afraid of any complications that might assail its simplistic criteria for evaluation. The fact, equally simple but more realistic, is that the greater the performer, the greater the liberties he can fruitfully take with the score – and the smaller the score, the greater they yet become. But even the greatest scores, when they face a truly great performer, willingly grant him the right of the foreground.

George Malcolm, in a radio talk I produced (actually it was a conversation between us, from which I removed my own contribution, unphoney editing for once!),* talked about 'the role of the performer in creation' and suggested that the act of composition did not finish with the composer having put down his score on paper – a genuinely creative point of view with which I absolutely concur, although two variables are, of course, involved in each particular case – the nature of the score and the nature of the performance. But even the greatest scores, seemingly executed to untouchable perfection, have, upon occasion, served as backgrounds for meticulously logical re-creative – no, *creative* foregrounds. Nor is the first example that occurs to me, as the reader might by now expect, one or the other interpretation of a Furtwängler or Huberman; it was a sober Englishman who, in my experience, went farthest in this direction – Reginald Kell, the clarinettist. Fortunately, at least one of his performances of great masterpieces, that of Mozart's Clarinet Quintet, is still available or, at any rate, inspectable on gramophone records, so the interested reader, and particularly the interested critic (if he has even read this far!) can check on the truth of my observations.

---

*See pp. 51ff.

What Reginald Kell, whom I heard in quite a few highly con-trasting interpretations of the work, achieved here in the way of creating a new foreground would not, in fact, have been accepted as a legitimate possibility by any of us without having actually heard the creative act. The most striking, meaningful contradic-tions of the background, i.e. the actual score, consisted in his doing dynamically the straight opposite of what Mozart had indicated or clearly implied. A phrase's main accent, that is to say, would be replaced by an unexpectable 'piano subito' – sensitively introduced by an infinitesimal hesitation, of course – with the result that the implied stress, the phrase's centre of gravity, was defined far more weightily than in any performance that followed the letter of the score more conscientiously. The composer, one felt certain, would have been delighted, and had his father not been dead by the time he wrote his Clarinet Quintet, he would have written him a long letter about Kell's performance – explaining, at the same time, why he could not insert Kell's dynamics and co-ordinated agogics in the score, for constant future use; his explanation, one feels equally sure, would have come jolly close to George Malcolm's reminder of the performer's compositional role.

The critic who wanted to judge how logically and how clearly the composer or performer had got his meanings across, how far he had said what he had to say, would either have to accept, at least in principle, our definition of the laws of musical thought and the laws of their operation, or else he would not only have to show us where we went wrong, but would also have to demonstrate to us how he supported his judgements analytically – what were his criteria of musical logicality which he invited us to accept. Otherwise, why should we listen to him, unless we accept his omniscience from the outset? Why should his personal preferences and prejudices, indeed his taste, be more interesting than yours? Because, maybe, he spent a lifetime, purely receptively, in the world of music? That might easily make his judgement worse, in proportion as it will have crystallized and calcified his taste.

Strictly speaking, I have now committed a grave pleonasm, but only for its identification to arouse the reader from his tasteful slumber, for what I am suggesting is that taste, far from being a valid part of the critic's (or teacher's) equipment, is an anti-artistic concept, much beloved by the critic who does not want to be bothered about the criteria of his judgement and is calmly proud of his superior sensitivity from the moment of its first appearance: all taste is still-born.

For while all meaningful art is, of necessity, about something new, all taste is, just as necessarily, about something old: taste depends on a measure of consensus, but discovery, including artistic discovery, which is all that art is about, precedes consensus. True enough, taste is established by works of art, but by the time it has established itself, art has moved on. Taste is therefore destined to limp behind, as the entire profession of criticism tends to do, whereas real art runs the continual risk of being regarded, to begin with, at any rate, as tasteless – before, that is, it in its turn contributes to reformulations of taste. It is thus that some of music's gigantic monuments, such as the finale of Beethoven's Ninth or indeed the Mahler symphonies, had to face, and turn their backs on, the charge of tastelessness. Nowadays, any post-Mahlerian, epigonic trash, on the other hand, is considered tasteful easily enough, since it meets the standards of taste which Mahler's music has meanwhile helped to crystallize – and calcify.

It seems that we have left the music critic little option, and the unanalytic critic virtually none. But on closer, rational inspection, the sky is not as cloudy as all that; 'broken cloud' would be a more sober weather report. For inasmuch as the critic is prepared to renounce omniscient and omnipotent violence, the sun may still shine on him and warm his heart, at least intermittently; he certainly needs it, or rather them – both a heart and the sun. Such a renunciation would of course mean that he would be prepared to be criticized himself, would even welcome criticism since he thinks so highly of the discipline. With a little more knowledge and insight, however – and the two, once initiated, move in a virtuous circle – he would find criticisms of his criticisms far less frightening, and the growth of inner authority would more than compensate him for the voluntary loss of that outer authority which institutionalized omniscience confers.

Judgement in newspaper criticism, to be sure, we appear to have proved impossible, but such an impossibility would not silence newspaper *reports* on musical events in general and new works in particular. Only, the writer would have to decide on an honest course of journalistic action, and if and when he could not refrain from expressing his distaste, he would have to make clear that personal distaste might mean as little as collective taste does. His editor, admittedly, would have to co-operate in any such attempt to free the musical atmosphere from time-honoured pollution. I well remember, from my early days in journalism, being reminded by editors that such phrases as, 'So far as I can hear . . .', 'In my own opinion . . .', 'I may be alone in thinking that . . .' were unprofessional: these things went as a matter of course, everybody knew that one only gave one's own opinion, there wasn't space for all these reservations which made for bad reading anyway, if I wasn't careful I would end up by starting every critical observation with the phrase, 'I think . . .'

Unfortunately, the truth usually is the last thing that goes as a matter of course, and once one has committed one's life to the black magic of print, one should be alive to the obligation to counteract it – its phonily objectifying effect. What a liberating, downright historic moment it would be for everybody concerned if, one sunny day, a notice on a new work started with the words, 'I don't know what to say.' Yet, innumerable are the occasions when the music critic doesn't know what to say – but the phonily professional conspiracy between him and his editor turns the suppression of an important, if negative truth into an act of skill which does not even scratch his, or his editor's conscience. If such an easy truth is not allowed to get out, what about the more difficult ones?

But if we can muster some tolerance towards the individual critic, inasmuch as he is prepared to let judgement take second place to analysis on the one hand and sheer reporting on the other – not to think of the occasional exceptional personality amongst critics that might be prepared to develop exquisitely rational group self-contempt – we simply see no artistic future for the profession of music criticism as it stands – and it has been standing still for an awfully long time. Group self-contempt we have carefully tucked away at a considerable distance from our peroration, such as it is, for if there is one mistake which this book wants to avoid, one trap into which many a worthier book has fallen, it is the eventual Utopian solution to problems well delineated, but ultimately unsolvable.

We have given the critic a hard time, but you, the public, deserve a hard time too, for without your co-operation, however passive, music criticism as we know it would long have ceased to exist, for the art of music can do splendidly without it – as is proved by all those musicians and music lovers, not inconsiderable in number, who hardly ever read music criticisms. But those who habitually do, show by their very interest that they identify with all that is phoney about the profession, with its lustful creation of unsolvable problems, its destructiveness, its omniscience, responsibility for which they therefore share by proxy.

It is for this reason that music criticism is sociologically inevitable without being artistically necessary, to put it as mildly as possible; I cannot think of any musician who would not agree that it is artistically superfluous. In any case – inevitability without necessity: can there be a problem more unsolvable? There is, of course, always the genius witch-pricker that never was; in fact, one would need quite a few of them. Let's leave a chair or two empty for them, like the Jews at Passover for the Messiah.

Postface

Well, I've made it, but the question remains what I have made. I finished the book last night, and during the night, though I normally sleep when I lie in bed, Kafka's diary entry about how he wrote 'The Judgement' (again a historic mistranslation:* it should be called 'The Verdict') in one night did not go out of my head – by way of contrast, not of megalomania: he must have known what he had made; in fact, he did. Not that I have any doubts; there won't be any second thoughts or revisions, because they would be third thoughts: I started the book on the basis of long-considered second thoughts. But what I have made depends, to some considerable extent, on the effect it will have – not on reviewers, but on the profession to which I have been a convinced traitor for decades. And there one might be a little pessimistic: the occasional second thought, fleeting, perhaps, might be all that one is realistically entitled to hope for.

When I was a little boy, I coined a maxim that proved utterly out of character, for which reason I'm proud of it, for it must have been conceived in one of those rare moments of dispassionate insight of which children, without daily 'real' worries, may be more easily capable than adults. I had watched the grown-ups hustling and bustling, urgently doing this and that, and making a mess of it half the time. This was when the downright eastern thought occurred to me. I rushed into the kitchen and said to my mother, in Viennese slang: 'Was ma nicht macht, is' gewonnen' – of which the closest possible translation is, 'Whatever you don't do is a gain.' And I went back into the garden, to continue what I described as thinking.

Would it have been a gain if I had not written this book? Only if it proved a dead loss, and that is impossible, because it is real: it is based on the protracted experience of that which it criticizes. This is the

---

*Cf. footnote on 'interpretation', p. 64.

reason, too, why it swerves to and fro between the impersonal and the personal. It may be thought that the fact that it was written in one go in three weeks is responsible for a degree of personal involvement that might otherwise not have manifested itself, but this is not so; the personal element had emphatically been planned before I put pen to paper, because in one respect the particular kind of person who wrote the book is of overriding importance: in the history of music criticism, if not of criticism as a whole, he is the first practitioner who has been consistently and articulately critical of the very craft he has practised. Nobody is unique, and for this reason alone, if for no other, he might not remain the last: it may not be a case of post-operational delusion to suggest that fleeting second thoughts will not, after all, be the last word in the matter, even if the chairs for the genius witch-prickers remain empty.

To music critics, certainly, my childhood maxim seems shatteringly relevant. Every single reader, one or two soft-boiled critics apart, will be able to think of at least one distinguished critic who would have deserved a top salary, and a relaxing pension, for remaining silent all his life. Once again, I speak with the corroboration of personal experience: the noblest critical achievements of my life were the moments when I decided to shut up, temporarily or, as in the case of most of the music of Debussy, Delius, and Sibelius, for ever. The amount of nonsense I have thus not committed to print, the violence and posthumous torture which has remained unpractised, would have made me a serious rival of the most highly-esteemed members of the profession if all those pseudo-thoughts, those thin rationalizations of incomprehension, had been allowed an outlet.

Fundamentally, the issue is as complex and as simple as that of *The Critique of Pure Reason*:* remove self-preoccupation and the only questions that remain are, first, whom and/or what do I harm or hurt and, secondly, can it be shown to be worth it? They are questions which, in their simplicity, go far beyond the problem of criticism: they embrace the whole of active life of which criticism, all criticism, is, in this respect, a focus. Not all you don't do may be a gain, but since activity tends to produce a good conscience, the morality of inactivity must needs be tragically ignored.

Lanzarote, 15 December 1976, 10.45 am.

---

*See p. 141.

Appendix

Note 1 (*re* footnote on p. 56)   This is one occasion where it has proved impossible to include material the author intended – namely, the review as he wrote it, in its *unedited* form. All searches for the original manuscript have unfortunately been in vain, and it has thus been necessary to change his introductory 'This is what I wrote' to 'Here is the review as it appeared.' As a consequence, a couple of minor alterations have also been made in the paragraphs which immediately follow the review; however, it is perfectly clear from the full description of his conversation with the *Guardian*'s Literary Editor, that the only loss to the present reader is the sentence concerning Elias Canetti, and even here, the gist of the author's original is not hard to fathom.

Note 2 (*re* footnote on p. 81)   While there is no doubt in my mind that this quote from Schopenhauer is the one the author intended, it was not included in the manuscript. He merely wrote: 'Schopenhauer conceived this beautiful thought:', and then left a blank page with 'my translation' written at the bottom. What is printed here is the result of an inspired idea of Leo Black, a friend and colleague of the author, who remembered this as one of his favourite Schopenhauer passages. Contextually, it is wholly apposite, and I am enormously indebted to Mr Black for his help. That I managed to find the author's own translation was extremely fortunate; it was published in a *Listener* article (23 May 1968) entitled 'Schopenhauer's Palestrina', in which he was previewing a forthcoming broadcast of Pfitzner's opera *Palestrina*. This Schopenhauer passage was used by the composer, the article told us, as 'motto for the opera'.

Note 3 (*re* footnote on p. 97)   The author introduces this review as 'a translated extract'. Again, this was not included with the manuscript; what is printed here is a full translation (obviously his own), which was found among his papers after his death. As far as I can ascertain, it has not been published in English before.